A User Guide to the GF/CF diet

of related interest

Diet Intervention and Autism
Implementing the Gluten Free and Casein Free Diet for Autistic Children and Adults – A Practical Guide for Parents
Marilyn Le Breton
Foreword by Rosemary Kessick, Allergy Induced Autism
ISBN 1 85302 935 1

The AiA Gluten and Dairy Free Cookbook
Marilyn Le Breton
Foreword by Rosemary Kessick, Allergy Induced Autism
ISBN 1 84310 067 3

Asperger's Syndrome
A Guide for Parents and Professionals
Tony Attwood
Foreword by Lorna Wing
ISBN 1 85302 577 1

Caring for a Child with Autism
A Practical Guide for Parents
Martine Ives and Nell Munro, National Autistic Society
ISBN 1 85302 996 3

A User Guide to the GF/CF Diet

For Autism, Asperger Syndrome and AD/HD

Luke Jackson

with appendices by Jacqui Jackson

Foreword by Marilyn Le Breton

Jessica Kingsley Publishers
London and Philadelphia

First published in the United Kingdom in 2002 by
Jessica Kingsley Publishers Ltd
116 Pentonville Road
London N1 9JB, England
and
325 Chestnut Street
Philadelphia, PA 19106, USA

www.jkp.com

Copyright © 2002 Luke Jackson
Copyright © 2002 Appendices Jacqui Jackson
Copyright © 2002 Foreword Marilyn Le Breton

Library of Congress Cataloging in Publication Data
A CIP catalog record for this book is available from the Library of Congress

British Library Cataloguing in Publication Data
A CIP catalogue record for this book is available from the British Library

ISBN 1 84310 055 X

Printed and Bound in Great Britain by
Athenaeum Press, Gateshead, Tyne and Wear

*This book is dedicated to my best
friend, my Mum*

Contents

Appendices

Foreword

When Jacqui told me that Luke was writing about his experiences of the diet, I thought, "Great. I wonder, if I ask really nicely, if Luke will let me read bits of it, when he's finished."

When Jacqui told me that JKP were going to publish his experiences, I mentally punched the air and shouted, "Yes!" out loud, to the bemusement of my family.

When, a few months later, Luke phoned and asked me if I would write the Foreword to his book, I choked back an emotional sob and tried to reply calmingly that I would be honoured and delighted to.

So why am I so excited about Luke's book? Well, by the time you have got to the end of the first page, you will be able to answer that question for yourself. Luke is incredibly articulate, charming, funny and disarmingly frank about his life and the effects of the diet. So this book is a completely absorbing and wonderful read.

But on a far more personal level, I was curious to find out about how it felt to be on the diet, what differences it made, what the 'withdrawal' was like and what life was like prior to the diet, from first-hand experience. I have been able to observe, with my son, Jack, the downright miraculous differences that the diet has made to every aspect of his life. But I could never, ever know what it felt like. My curiosity has been further fuelled by a few remarks that Jack has been making recently. He has refused some foods stating, "No thank you, it will make my tummy hurt/make me sick." Some of the foods that he had eaten pre-diet with relish (but now off-limits), he has seen and stated very calmly, "I used to eat that; it made my tummy/head hurt." Jack is five and a half years old and has been on the diet for a little over two years. I am amazed that he can remember that certain foods made him feel bad, especially as pre-diet, he was so severely autistic, I did not think he was aware of surroundings, let alone able to make the link that certain foods made him 'ill'. Luke has helped me to fill in the gaps, until Jack is able to do this for himself – of which I have no doubt that he will do one day.

I was also fascinated to read how different foods and additives had completely different adverse effects upon Luke, Joe and Ben. Here are three brothers, all at different points on the autistic spectrum, all benefiting from the diet, but each markedly different in how different foods and additives made them feel and how the diet has affected them. Luke's ability to observe his brothers and re-count their stories will help other families enormously and has already helped me when talking to parents who phone the AiA help-line. I am constantly being asked, "Will this diet help my child? Isn't he too old/he's only mildly autistic/he's Aspergers/ he has ADHD." After reading Luke's book, so much becomes clearer.

Luke's book is a fascinating read: for every parent who has a child on the diet, for every parent contemplating implementing the diet with their child and for professionals everywhere who deal with people on the autistic spectrum.

So I would like to thank Luke, for taking the time and the trouble to write this brilliant book. I have learnt so much from Luke's book and I am sure that many other people will learn a lot too. I also think that he is a very special person for trying to help other people. I sincerely hope that this will not be the last book that you have published. I would also like to end (finally) by quoting Luke:

"I think that a parent should do all they can to try to help their child with any difficulties they have and so should at least give this diet a go."

A sentiment echoed by myself and all at AiA.

Marilyn Le Breton
August 2001

Acknowledgements

I would like to use this opportunity to thank these people in public.

- To know that I am not a 'freak' and to find that there is a reason why I have always felt different is one of the greatest reliefs of my life. For this I would like to thank Julia Leach (Educational psychologist) for caring enough to send Mum an article to show me and encourage her that it was time to tell my brothers, sisters, and I that I had Asperger Syndrome.

- Thank you to Marilyn Le Breton for encouraging me when I was fed up and for giving Mum so much help and information when she was learning about the diet.

- Thank you to Barbara from Barbara's kitchen for all her recipes that make the GF/CF diet more bearable and helping Mum to bake so well.

- Thank you to each one of my brothers and sister for adding something special to my life; Matthew for being a wonderful big brother – always there for me; Rachel and Sarah for helping me when times were tough and for trying to understand; Anna for helping with baking and accepting me for who I am; Joe for cheering me up and making me laugh; and Ben for lighting up all of our lives

- Thank you to Grandad and Margaret, Aunty Heather, Uncle Steve, my wonderful cousin Sammy, Uncle Colin and Philippa and Granny for accepting me as I am, funny quirks and all!

- Thank you to my learning support teacher, Heather Brookman, for providing my word processor and helping me so much with work and other matters.
- Thank you to Jessica for believing in my capabilities and making this book a reality.

1

The Autistic Spectrum and the Diet

Over recent years there has been a growing awareness concerning the autistic spectrum but diagnosis criteria still vary enormously. It is however, widely accepted that people on the autistic spectrum have difficulties in the area of language, communication, social interaction and imagination and often engage in obsessive or repetitive behaviours and rituals. Many people on the spectrum also suffer from debilitating stomach and bowel problems. There is increasing evidence that the removal of the 'intoxicating' effects of gluten and casein by implementing a gluten and casein free diet, can result in remarkable benefits in many of these areas. Convinced that the diet was worth a try with my family I embarked on our GF/CF journey. The outcome has surpassed my wildest expectations.

The spectrum includes both people who are severely affected and may be non-verbal, and those at the other end of the spectrum people with high functioning autism (HFA) and Asperger Syndrome (AS). Attention deficit, hyperactivity disorder is identified by a rather different set of diagnostic criteria, but is increasingly recognised as, at the least, a related condition.

Diagnostic difficulties often arise especially at the high-functioning end of the spectrum. Who is it that actually defines a problem in any one given area? Does a child who approaches a stranger and kisses his or her legs have a problem with social interaction, or is there only a problem when the child is withdrawn and reserved? If someone feels different and isolated inside, but has learned the rules of the game and can behave 'sociably', does he have a problem? Does someone who is perfectly happy with her own company and with being alone have a problem at all? There are now many books that delve into these issues. I work on the premise that, if something constitutes a problem for the individual him- or herself, then it is indeed a problem.

One area of ongoing debate concerns intervention with the intention to normalise. Many people on the spectrum or with a child with these 'conditions' are clear that many aspects are beautiful, unique and to be cherished. Luke writes of his concerns, even annoyance, that this diet was 'devised' with the sole aim of eradicating all aspects of autistic spectrum disorders and he was, initially, exceedingly disgruntled!

Nevertheless, many areas are indeed disabling, and it is those areas that we should seek to eradicate or ameliorate. I know only too well the feeling of desperation and the desire to reach your apparently unreachable child, the feeling of helplessness you experience as your child suffers with disabling stomach and bowel problems.

The GF/CF diet has enabled many, many people to 'connect' with the world in which we live in a much clearer way. For Luke and others with Asperger Syndrome, that connection has led to a much deeper understanding of himself and the social world.

The GF/CF diet, is not a 'cure' for autism, Asperger Syndrome or AD/HD. It may not work for everyone, it may not have the same effect for everyone, but, as Luke says, you will never know unless you give it a try!

– Jacqui Jackson

2

Introduction to *Moi*

My name is Luke Jackson. I am twelve years old, I have Asperger Syndrome (AS) and I am on a gluten and casein free diet (GF/CF). If you are not sure what either of those are, then I hope you will read on and will understand more fully by the end of the book.

I have written this book for a few reasons. People often tell me how polite I am and I do try to be helpful. I am hoping that this book will encourage parents to learn more and understand what the GF/CF diet can do for a child with autism, AD/HD or Asperger Syndrome. I think that a parent should do all they can to try to help their child with any difficulties they have and so should at least give this diet a go.

I also know that there are some people with autism who do not speak. They may choose not to or may be unable to. If these children are on the GF/CF diet, I would like to be their 'voice' and let their parents know that just because they have not started chattering away, it does not mean the diet has had no effect on them. I hope I can help lots of parents to understand their child a little better.

I also know what some people will be thinking when they read this. You will be thinking, "Does this diet work for people with AS too?" The answer to that is "yes". No one is ever too 'mild' or too old.

One thing that really annoys me is that Asperger Syndrome is often called a milder form of autism. I actually find that quite insulting, although I do understand that people have to explain it somehow.

I like to think of the autistic spectrum as one long line with people dotted about the line. I am sure there are many undiagnosed people who are on that line somewhere and feel different from others but maybe are not sure of the reason why. One example of this is my brother Joe. He has all the characteristics of AD/HD. He has real problems with listening and concentrating and he is hyperactive and impulsive but he also has some funny little ways that are very like other autistic people I know. To us he is just Joe, but he is definitely somewhere along that line and knowing that makes it easier for us to understand him.

I like computers and we have one at home, which has a HP DeskJet six-sixty printer and a 56K modem. I used it for quite a lot of things, ranging from homework to making web pages but now I only use it for the Internet because I have my own laptop now. I like making web sites.

My family consists of eight people: my Mum who is thirty seven and five months, Matthew who is seventeen and eight months, Rachel who is fifteen and ten months, Sarah who is fourteen and two months, Anna who is eleven and one month, Joseph who is eight and two months, Ben who is four and three quarters, and me. Of course everyone's age will have changed slightly when this is published but not enough to matter really.

I attend Arnold Private Senior School and my favourite subjects there are French, Latin, German and, of course, IT. I moved from my last secondary school because I was getting bullied. Things are much better where I am now.

I go to a thing called 'learning support' which helps me with crowds and remembering things, generally things to do with Asperger syndrome. The teacher, Heather Brookman, is really nice and helps me a lot.

I also go to a Taekwondo class at Blackpool Sports Centre, which is run by Master Craig Waddington who is sixth Dan (that's well up from a black belt). It is the ILGI Taekwondo association – IL means one and GI means together – I think that's a cool name. I am usually alone so it is nice to think of myself as together as one with others who do Taekwondo. It is really enjoyable and helps me get fit and confident and it improves my reflexes. It is also good if you get into a sticky situation somewhere, as you can defend yourself.

I have also been looking for a relaxation club, like Yoga, but I found out you can only attend Yoga when you are fourteen because the bones are not developed. I'll keep looking anyhow.

That is enough about me.

I have compared doing this diet with a boat journey – a bit rough, a few accidents, but it is worth it because you end up at a much better place.

3

The Diet in a Nutshell[*]

A bit of basic biology

First of all I have to say that although I am not your 'regular' kid – I am only 12 years old and I am no child prodigy, so do not profess to know as much as others about the theory behind the diet – I will explain what I know and point you in the right direction to get information about the diet. There are plenty of addresses and links at the back of the book, where you will be able to learn more.

Some people cannot break down gluten and so it damages the intestine and causes big problems. Joe is like that. This is called coeliac disease and the treatment for that is a gluten free diet forever. The problems autistic people have with gluten are not the same as this, though many autistic people have coeliac disease as well.

There are physical signs that someone has a problem with gluten and casein and may benefit from the diet and I will list a few, but that doesn't mean that, if none are present, then the diet won't work, or that anyone has to have them all. Here are the ones that were obvious in our family and I am sure that there are more:

---

* (I do so love these ridiculous expressions.)

- constant craving for gluten and/or dairy foods
- pale face
- black rings around the eyes
- red ears or one red ear
- bloated stomach
- excessive thirst
- excessive sweating
- poor sleeping habits
- behavioural problems
- diarrhoea
- constipation
- excessive wind (He he!)
- seems unable to feel pain.

Here is my attempt at an explanation of the theory behind this diet and though it is not so detailed, I think it is accurate. I am not the kind of person that likes to give out false information.

The theory, still being researched, is that people on the autistic spectrum do not completely break down gluten and casein. Gluten is the protein found in most grains (four actually) and casein is the protein found in dairy produce. Because these proteins are not broken down properly, they end up as little bits called peptides. These peptides pass through the wall of the stomach, which is often damaged and 'leaky' in kids like me (hence the fact that most of us have stomach problems, such as constipation or diarrhoea). Gluten breaks down into a peptide called gluteomorphine and casein breaks down into a peptide called caseomorphorphine. These peptides whizz around the body and cause people to become literally addicted to them. As you can guess by the name, these have the effect of morphine (or heroin). By removing the offending foods (those which contain gluten and casein) from your or your child's diet, the production of these peptides stops and so the 'heroin' effect stops too, resulting in changes in behaviour (for the better).

I must admit that I cannot remember ever feeling 'high' after eating bread or drinking milk but I do remember my little brother Ben being exactly that. He giggled hysterically at nothing and flicked his fingers in front of his face. He always seemed drugged; that was what made Mum start searching for answers to why he was always laughing.

So what is the problem with getting a quick fix out of foods? Some people may even be envious!

Well the trouble with that is, the times when the body isn't getting its drug, it goes into a withdrawal and then the addict feels ghastly, usually sweating, being dreadfully thirsty and having behavioural problems.

As I am older, I don't go around banging my head and screaming the place down, but apparently I used to be like that for years.
Joe goes really wild and hyper and Ben has massive tantrums.

After the peptides have whizzed about the body and muddled
up the brain causing all sorts of strange behaviours, they eventually pass through the body and out in the urine.

We had urine analysis done by Paul Shattock at the Autism
Research Unit (see Useful Information and Websites at the end of
the book). He analyses the urine to see if the peptides are present.
In mine the peptides for both gluten and casein were there. Ben's
urine analysis was not as they expected it to be but the diet has certainly changed his life. Joe's analysis showed that he had a severe
leaky gut. His results looked like the Himalayas!

The only trouble, I reckon, with this analysis, is that sometimes
the peptides are not present, for whatever reason and then maybe
someone thinks the diet would not be worthwhile. I think that it is
worth a try anyway because no one knows till they try whether or
not the diet will have any effect.

All in all though, I would say, leave the research to carry on and
give the diet a try. There is nothing at all to lose and loads to gain.

Gluten and casein

Some people may not be sure what things have gluten and casein
in. I hadn't even heard of gluten or casein before I started the diet,
so some other people might not either. When I started the diet,
though, I learnt that almost every food I was eating had gluten and
casein in, though with all of them it had been cleverly disguised in
other ingredients. I couldn't give you a list of everything with
gluten or casein in, as it would take up a whole chapter easily, but
don't let this put you off. There are some great books that can list
all you need to watch for (see Further Reading) but here are the
most common ones. Even Joe knows to look for these.

- Casein, caseinate, or anything with the word casein in it.

- Lactose and anything with the word lactose or 'lact' in it; there are some really complicated ones, like lactalbumin phosphorate (just thought I'd show off that I know that one!). Now I have said that, I must contradict myself and mention lactic acid. This always confused me so I have now thoroughly researched it. It seems that lactic acid is produced from the fermentation of sugar, milk or corn. Our muscles also produce small amounts of it as they split and expand. I have a joke; if GF/CF people produce this then do we produce 'soytic acid' or 'ricetic acid'? Anyway it seems that if it says 'lactic acid' on the ingredient list and also 'milk free' then it is derived from another product.

- Milk and anything with the word milk in it.

- Whey and anything with the word whey in it.

- Gluten

- Barley or any barley stuff.

- Malt: syrups, flavouring, extract, vinegar. Nothing with malt in is acceptable even though it often says suitable for a gluten free diet. Coeliacs can have the traces that we can't.

- Oats; some coeliacs can have oats but we can't.

- Rye and all rye stuff.

- Spelt (I am not sure what it is but I do know to look for it and we can't have it)

- Wheat or anything with the word wheat in it. Wheat syrup, wheat starch – the lot are all out.

Although this list and especially the full ones in other books look long, you soon get to know what products have what in and then this cuts down on your 'reading' time next time you go shopping. Mum usually does the shopping over the Internet and knows pretty much what we can have (Ben will not go shopping!) but if we do go together, all of us know what to look for and it really is not too bad.

Foods to avoid

There are full lists of what is in what and what to avoid in other books, but here are some very obvious things that will need substituting:

- butter
- beef burgers
- bread
- biscuits
- cakes
- cereal (most contain malt extract)
- cheese
- chicken nuggets (there aren't any GF/CF chicken nuggets you can buy that I know of but Mum does make them)
- chocolate
- cream
- crisps (most contain msg – see below)
- gravy granules (I don't think there are any but Mum does it with meat juices and GF/CF flour)
- milk

- pasta
- sausages
- squash (most contain aspartame – see below)
- yoghurt.

All these things can be replaced easily enough apart from breaded stuff like chicken nuggets. Mum does chicken pieces in a batter stuff and those are much better so I am not complaining. The packaging of everything else you buy needs reading because some things have the offenders in and some don't. You soon learn. Things you wouldn't expect have offending stuff in too, so you need to watch out for washing up liquid and dishwasher tablets and shampoo and stuff. These are not the major things to worry about at first but you will definitely react to those little bits once you have cleared the gluten and casein out of your system.

Monosodium glutamate and aspartame

Now a word about monosodium glutamate and aspartame. Aspartame is an artificial sweetener and is easily identified but monosodium glutamate, which is a flavour enhancer, is hidden in crafty ways. It is E621, flavour enhancer or msg and is in hydrolysed vegetable protein, gelatine, yeast extract and probably other stuff that I am afraid I don't know. These are the ones I look for and are the most common. There are links about this at the end of the book. I know very little about these apart from the fact that they are called 'excito toxins' which indicates to me that they 'excite' the brain and are toxic. It doesn't take a genius to work that out!

I think that some people do the GF/CF diet and still have these in their diet, but I can tell you from watching my brothers in particular, that they make one big difference to their behaviour. These are the things that Ben and Joe react to immediately. As I have said, for more information on all this stuff, there are references and links at the end of the book that will go into more detail that I ever can.

What I can tell you that they can't is what it is like to have this stuff inside you and what you or your child may feel like when you remove it. The headaches, which come along with monosodium glutamate and aspartame, are awful. I wonder if lots of people have these and don't even realise that it is affecting them?

4

So What's in It for Me?

(Or Your Child of Course!)

"You know when you look at a picture and it looks very flat and boring and then when you look closely there's all sorts of interesting stuff in it? Well that's what it's like when you're not on this diet and then you go on it. Everything seems really boring but when your mum puts you on a proper diet, everything around becomes exciting and there's lots more stuff in the world after all!"

–Joe Jackson

Is it really worth the bother?

That is the million dollar question. Is this diet really worth all the bother? Well I think you may guess my answer to that one but I will try to tell you why a bit more fully.

Gluten takes about eight or nine months to get out of someone's system properly, but casein only takes about three days. Although I am pretty good at science, I am not a scientist so all the biological stuff can be gone into more deeply by looking at other people's work. All I know properly is that it does help.

Enduring the period before the gluten goes completely and not 'giving in' to eating gluten foods and dairy stuff is rewarding.

It gives a sense of achievement and personally it makes me feel as if I am taking control of my own life. I think this is important for people with AS.

Throughout my infants and junior school, bullies have always picked on me. Whether I ignored them or told adults about it, it always started up again. Some kids just seem to get singled out because they are different. When I went to a senior school, the bullying there was so bad that Mum stopped me going to that school and now I go to Arnold senior school. The bullying started there too but Mrs Nichols and my Mum sorted it out pretty quickly. I must say that Mum did 'mention' that I did Taekwondo to the bullies, saying how dangerous I could be. I think that helped!

The GF/CF diet has enabled me to think a lot more clearly, and feel healthier and more confident about who I am. This is an important part of making a stand against bullies. I would think that a very important reason for putting your child on the diet would be the feeling that you are doing something positive. After all, no parent wants to say 'well that is it, my son or daughter will have stomach ache and be oblivious to the world for the rest of their life'. I can't speak for parents of course, but I would think that most would want to do all they could to help their children have a better life.

Trying your child on a GF/CF diet and cutting out monosodium glutamate and aspartame is something that can be done without doing anything harmful. It's not as if you are going to inject your child with potentially harmful stuff or give them drugs without knowing exactly what side effects there are going to be. If the diet is done properly, it is healthy and the food is just like any other food. In general most of it is nicer than before, though of course there will always be some things that each individual doesn't like. That is the same for everyone I believe. One of my sisters really hates pasta and cheese sauce and one of them is absolutely mad on it. That just shows how different people are.

What changes?

My brother Joe is eight, has attention and listening problems and is hyperactive. I would say that is AD/HD, but whether that is his diagnosis I don't know. He has been doing the diet since he was two because he had really bad diarrhoea and was sick loads. He gets very wheezy after he has had milk stuff and is on the loo all night after eating gluten. His behaviour is wild with gluten too and he is moody and nasty with dairy stuff. It was only when we took out things such as malt extract, oats, monosodium glutamate, aspartame and artificial colourings and preservatives that he really stopped being so hyperactive.

It was a huge change; he went from being a boy who ripped off his wallpaper and split his pillows open to asking Mum if she wanted a cup of tea (which is a real pain because he then asks someone else to make her one, but I suppose it is the thought that counts!) and cleaning and tidying the bathroom.

My little brother Ben is on the diet too. He is four and is autistic. Bread has the effect of morphine on him and he gets 'high' from eating it. All he ate was toast, toast and more toast. He used to ignore everyone and close his eyes, look up at the ceiling and laugh hysterically. Now he pays full attention to everyone and has stopped being so 'autistic'. He knows when Mum is in or out of the room and often screams for her to come back. He talks more and more each day and has some really funny expressions, though he is still very hard to understand. It makes me laugh just to think of the things he says and does.

Before the diet, his laughing was infectious and made everyone laugh but it was also kind of sad, because he didn't know we were there or were laughing. Mum used to spend forever, doing stupid things to get him to notice her and he never did.

Before the diet I had huge black rings around my eyes going right down to the tip of my nose. Now these are gone and only come back after an infringement of the diet. Your child will have to be very careful not to eat any 'off limit' foods. Sometimes there are hidden offenders in even supposedly gluten free foods, so you may have to phone the manufacturer, although there is loads of information about to help so that isn't necessary very often.

Now here is something that I find pretty ironic. I started the diet initially because I have always had such problems getting to sleep and staying asleep. Everything I had read about it said that it helped sleep problems. Never a day goes by when someone doesn't comment on how tired I look or how I look like 'death warmed up'. It gets annoying I can tell you! Anyway, Joe was so hyper that he never slept and sneaked around the house trying to nick foods all night and Ben laughed hysterically and spun things around on his feet all the time (a clever trick spinning a Fisher Price garage around on his feet when it was as big as him) so they didn't sleep either.

The diet calmed Joe down and he now sleeps really well, just playing with little models and things till he falls asleep. Ben goes to sleep well now, though doesn't often stay asleep, and the giggling has stopped completely.

Well my brothers' sleep problems were made much better. Now to my sleep problems – guess what? I still have them!

Now don't read this and think that the diet isn't worth doing. That just isn't true, it is, but it didn't solve my sleep problems and I think it is only fair and honest to say that.

There may be some parts of you or your child that the diet may not help or change. Maybe they are not meant to be changed. People don't comment on how tired I look any more and how ill I look, so they presume I sleep better. Maybe I am just one of those people who doesn't need to sleep much, but I sure would like to find a way to get to sleep. So far Mum has tried relaxation techniques, aromatherapy, lavender oil, homeopathic stuff and all sorts of traditional drugs that the GP recommended.

I used to have stomach pains and diarrhoea all the time, completely non-stop because I was eating gluten foods so regularly. I hardly ever have them now because I only ever eat gluten accidentally, so I'm hardly ever ill. That is the same for Joe, though he still takes foods he shouldn't have if he gets half a chance. He seems to think suffering by sitting on the loo all night is worth it, just to get a quick 'fix' of gluten or casein.

Ben had the opposite problem to us. He has always been constipated. He has had a 'poo nurse' who has come out to him ever since he was a tiny baby. She gave him enemas and advised Mum about his laxatives. He used to get in such a state trying to poo, that loads of times he had to be taken up to the hospital for them to try to get it out. (A bit of a disgusting topic but it is relevant.) He now poos absolutely fine, smears it all over, in fact, and Mum often says that she is not bothered because she is still so delighted that he can go on his own without bleeding and being in such pain.

While I am on the subject of poo, I may as well continue in this rather disgusting way and tell you that my sisters always said my breath smelt like it! I know that sounds awful and I sure got sick of it, but everyone said my breath stank. Personally I couldn't really care, but then I am not the sort of kid who bothers about other people's opinions (I think Mum would like the GF/CF diet to make me wash more too!) but my family don't comment on my breath now and everyone says that the smell has gone. If I have had an infringement the smell comes back but nowhere near as bad as pre-diet.

Those are just some little examples of how changing our diet has had beneficial effects on my brothers and me. One thing I can say is that it is definitely worth a try for you or your child. It needs a decent length of time before you can safely say that it has not worked. I would recommend a year, but at least eight months, anyway. I would say that if you can help yourself or you child one bit then you should do it. For some people the diet has been miraculous; for others it has helped or changed them gradually. Whichever way, it needs to be done one hundred per cent; there are no half measures. People often say, 'a little bit won't harm', well it certainly will. Remember that.

Starting Out – The Journey Begins

First things first – clearing the decks

Starting the diet is a good time to clean the kitchen and throw out all those things that you never use. Mind you, Mum would say that any time is a good time to clean the kitchen.

From now on, any breadcrumbs in the food and you'd better have your toilet roll at the ready; it takes many torturous days (most of them spent in the lavatory!) to get any gluten out of your system.

Turn the kitchen into a GF/CF version of a 'kosher' kitchen (that is what it is really; all the pots and pans split into gluten free and normal), and have at least one area that is completely GF/CF. One side of our kitchen is strictly to be used for GF/CF foods. We have our own cupboards and work surface and anyone who uses that side (in most cases Anna, my sister) gets the blame for making us ill.

Buy another toaster, bread bin and chopping board and sort the cupboards so that all the GF/CF food is readily available and the other stuff is not. I know that sounds expensive, but you only have to do it once and, if you don't, all the hard work will be wasted.

Does everyone have to do it?

If possible, all go GF/CF. It is much better for those on the diet if there is no temptation and, for those young children or children who do not understand, it is far better to have nothing around that they can get their hands on.

The diet is healthy and tasty, but if the rest of the family doesn't want to go GF/CF, then it is good to do as we do, and make the main meal GF/CF so that all the family can eat together. There are many meals that everyone will like.

We all like lasagne and Mum can even fool Matthew my elder brother into believing it is not GF/CF. Actually he made a pretty good GF/CF lasagne himself once and didn't contaminate anything.

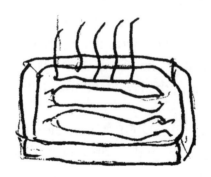

He literally lives on Minstrels, Cherry Coke and prawn cocktail crisps. That is his diet. He is dyslexic, actually, and there is some evidence that dyslexic people would benefit from the GF/CF diet…but there is no chance that Mat would ever eat our 'skanky' food. He is really funny because he says that and then goes and eats about ten biscuits that Mum has just baked.

We all actually eat much better now than we did before, and a lot more. Then again, I'm not complaining. Mum is the best cook I've ever seen.

How and when

The next thing you need to do is decide how you are going to do the diet and when you are going to start it.

I would say that a lot of people think and talk about this task too much, but then I am not the one who does the cooking. Maybe for a parent it is more difficult to decide to do, whether it is for them or their child. One thing I can say though, is there will never be just the right time to start this diet, so it may as well be now. Remember that just one more food with gluten or casein in it is one more fix of gluteomorphine and caseomorphine to get rid of, and with every fix you get more addicted. It's better just to give the diet a go as soon as you can.

Some people go 'cold turkey' (I believe that is an expression that people use to describe when a drug user suddenly stops using) which is what we did. We also removed gluten and casein together although Paul Shattock from the Autism Research Unit in Sunderland advises doing them separately. I can see how this is the logical way to do it, because if someone reacted to gluten and not casein or vice versa, then they wouldn't be able to tell if they took them both out at once.

I had had the urine analysis done which showed both a gluten and a casein peak so I was pretty sure anyway, that they both needed to be removed. Joseph had already had gluten and casein removed from his diet so it was easier for us all to be the same. I reckon Mum is too impatient as well. I think once parents eventually decide to do this, they probably want to do the lot in one go.

If you are deciding to remove things gradually and wean yourself or your child off gluten and casein, then decide when you are going to remove them and what you are going to replace them with. If your child is hooked on one particular gluten or casein food, then you could just cut out one lot and substitute with the nearest gluten or casein free alternative, then the next day or day after, substitute another, till they are right down on their gluten or casein intake.

You can either try and make GF/CF foods as like, in taste and looks, to the gluten and casein foods as you can, or you can just go for something completely different. Which you do depends on whether your child will alter what they eat or whether he or she is set in their ways.

Personally I would suggest just 'going for it' rather than weaning yourself or your child off, because that just prolongs the withdrawals, but I suppose that is a matter of choice.

Withdrawals – the storm before the calm!

> "When you stop all bad foods it takes a few many days before your tummy stops hurting and you stop having diarrhoea all the time. Things smell funny and you feel really nervous and silly and can't stop it and you really feel like rice crispies a very lot. Ben bangs his head all the time when he wants bread but now he can walk and nearly talk."

> *–Joe Jackson*

It seems fairly obvious to me that if someone is 'addicted' to gluten and casein, when these 'drugs' are taken away, the body is going to react to being without them. This is the hard part and the bit that will worry a lot of parents or people thinking of starting the diet. It takes some willpower to resist the temptation to eat off limit food or not to give in to your child's desperation.

Different people react in different ways to this and everyone is different. To tell you the truth it's a hard time to cope with, but if you stick to the diet you will be rewarded. I would really hate to put anyone off starting the diet, but I think it is only fair to say that there can be many symptoms of gluten and casein withdrawal.

Here are some symptoms of withdrawal that people may experience. I hope this won't make you think that you feel things that just aren't there, or presume your child is experiencing this when they are not. It is only a guide. It is rather like reading the side effects of medicines – it is better to list them all but you may get none

- stomach cramps
- diarrhoea
- hyperactivity
- aggression
- depression
- forgetfulness
- light-headedness
- poor concentration
- spots
- joint pains
- headaches
- feeling as if you are in a trance
- feeling lethargic
- changes in sensitivities (all or any of the senses).

I also had a massive drop in the standard of my schoolwork, to such an extent that the school called my mum in to ask if there was anything wrong. I didn't follow my own advice then and tell the school and others that I was starting the diet.

There may be other symptoms too, but this certainly does not mean that you or your child is going to get them all. It is a good idea to know what a child may be feeling if they cannot talk, though. It will help you be more tolerant. I know that some children have really bad behaviour.

Here's how the withdrawals affected my brothers and me.

Joe was much more hyperactive than usual, he was destructive and aggressive, he jumped about and destroyed anything that came within two metres of him, and he definitely had far worse concentration. He really got on everyone's nerves, but I suppose we couldn't blame him. He had stomach ache and diarrhoea too. After about five days of real craziness and the maddest, wildest, hyperactivity I have ever seen in him, he suddenly went quiet. That was a real shock! Joe is never quiet and never sits still and all of a sudden there he was sitting and biting his nails with a really pale face and looking like he was so, so sad. Mum kept looking at him and I knew it upset her. After one day like that, she even said that she would rather have the old Joe back. I am not sure it bothered me that much but it was kind of weird. He was like Tigger when he lost his bounce. All in all it took about a week to ten days for Joe to get back to his noisy, but not so hyper as usual, self.

Ben refused to eat anything at all for the first two days. The only thing he did was drink Soya milk and he has always had that, so it was no change for him. Mum tried to tempt him in so many ways but he ate nothing. I think that this is a clever way of black-mailing parents into giving them gluten and casein foods. Ben is quite crafty I think. I reckon he knows a lot more than he lets on.

After two days he began to eat rice cakes and GF/CF cornflakes.

Remember that those little bits of malt extract really do make the difference, so Kellogg's and ordinary brands of cereal are out, even if they say gluten free.

He then got very angry and had mad cravings for all gluten foods (we all did!). We had to keep the kitchen door locked at all times and he just lay by it, screaming and having tantrums. He did loads of head banging and had terrible diarrhoea – he is usually constipated so I think Mum was glad about that bit.

This time for me was not so obvious but seemed to take longer. I wonder whether that is to do with me having gluten and casein in my system for much longer or because of the fact that I have Asperger's Syndrome rather than autism or hyperactivity. Whatever the reason, I felt pretty horrid.

I felt really depressed and felt like just curling up into a little ball. I just withdrew into my own little shell, wishing the ground would swallow me up – and hoping the toilet wouldn't! I had really bad diarrhoea and stomach pains (I think we all did) and just sat down at the computer or the Playstation most of the time. My schoolwork went down loads but I still didn't tell the school. That was something I really should have done. I felt like I was looking at everything from the outside in and I couldn't remember anything for more than about an hour. It was horrible while it lasted, but do try to remember that it does pass. For me it took just over two weeks to start feeling better again but then again, everyone is different so I couldn't really say how long this lasts.

The black rings around my eyes were still there and I still looked like 'death warmed up', but everyone said that they didn't think the rings were quite so bad. They did take months to go completely, so don't think the diet is not working if black rings around the eyes are still prominent.

After the initial pain, all of us were ravenous and felt as if we hadn't eaten for weeks on end. It was horrible, we got desperate for food and started to eat anything we found that was even remotely edible, though for Ben it didn't have to be edible at all – he started to eat the telephone wire and everything that came into contact with his mouth! He still licks and chews all sorts of weird things, but nowhere near as much as he used to.

If you are doing this with a small child or have the chance to do this yourself, I advise just locking the doors, switching off the telephone and getting it over with.

Coping with the withdrawals – a few helpful hints

In an ideal world, I would say keep away all visitors, throw away any gluten and casein foods and just do it…but this world is far from ideal and, for most people, that just isn't possible.

Now some of this, all of this, or none of this may be applicable to you but it is better to be prepared, I would say. No one can know what withdrawing will be like for any one person, but remember one thing – it is a very positive sign.

If you or your child is experiencing anything other than everyday life, then it is very probable that the body is reacting to the removal of gluten and casein. This is a VERY good thing.

By that I don't mean that the withdrawing is a good thing – it certainly is not, but the fact that there is a reaction is a sure sign that there will be an improvement when the body has got rid of the offending drugs (I hope you don't consider me too blunt).

Here are some tips to help you cope. I am sure you will find your own ways too but these helped us.

Helpful hints for all

- The first thing you do need to do if you are doing this with your child or for yourself, is to tell family, friends and schoolteachers that you are doing this diet. This is very important. I didn't do this, and they were very worried, I think, because I went from getting eighteen out of eighteen in my Latin tests, to getting one out of eighteen. The withdrawals seem to muddle up your brain for a while, but it is only temporary so don't worry. I am back to my usual self now.

- Prepare your explanation of the diet. It is often quite difficult to explain about this diet, so if you don't want to go into details you can just tell them you are allergic to some foods and will be ill for a while whilst it gets out of yours or your child's system.

- For those of you with small children, make sure you always have a supply of suitable foods to give to the nursery, school or wherever. It is no use going though the withdrawals only to find that someone has given your child something that they should not eat.

- Don't go to a great effort to make fancy GF/CF meals at this time, as they will probably not be eaten. Mum did this. What a waste of time and money that was! On the first day she made all sorts of stuff and Ben refused to eat it and Joe and I had stomach ache and felt sick.

- Don't bother with trying to eat or get your child to eat bread because even though there are some decent substitutes that you can get on prescription, it doesn't taste like ordinary bread. You should save gluten free bread for when the withdrawals have finished and you have perfected making it. It takes a long time to get right but tastes gorgeous when it is warm and done perfectly.

- Make each meal something to look forward to and try to make a filling breakfast. Waffles are good and you can get a waffle-maker and just dump the mix into that.

- Have loads of GF/CF snacks available. Mum does bake biscuits and cakes, but we get biscuits on prescription and take those in packed lunches. These sometimes leave a strange, powdery sensation on the roof of your mouth, but don't let this put you off, they are nice overall and you soon get used to it.

Tips for parents of smaller or less able autistic kids

- If the child is really mobile, then lock the kitchen door or at least lock away all off limit foods. We lock the kitchen door.

- Move out of reach anything that you don't want broken. The best thing to do is move away anything at all that can be thrown. Ben got quite angry and chucked things around all over the place.

- Move things that the child is likely to hurt themselves on too. Ben did quite a bit of throwing himself to the floor and head banging in the earlier stages. Make sure there is space for safe tantrums.

- Prepare yourself and expect to have broken sleep and some bad days. Try to have as few other things to do as possible and get some early nights before you stop the offending foods.

- Have a supply of favourite things ready. Mum got Ben loads of 'autistic' toys that he is really into, like dominos and bricks to line up and beads to push around a wire. Ben is really into lining up and putting things in and out of containers for ages and is usually only allowed to do this at some times in the day. When she removed his beloved toast from him, she let him do all this kind of stuff as much as he wanted to.

- Have a good supply of nappies and cream available. Running out to the shops with a screaming autistic child with diarrhoea is no fun – we have done it!

- Have a 'safe place' for your child to go. We have someone called Mick Conelly in our area who knows all about AS and ASD and he suggested we got a massive cardboard box for Ben to go in because he always goes under the quilts or behind the settee. It would be really good idea to get that before you started the withdrawals. I know it sounds weird but it works.

For those with AS or parents of kids with AS

- It would be better if you could start the diet at a time when you are free to do what you want and have as few distractions as possible. School holidays or some time off work would be the best time.

- If you are going to start the diet with an older child with AS, then talk to them first and let them read all they can about the theory behind all this. I am sure they would like to feel better too and understanding things make it much easier to follow the diet.

- Be prepared to feel rough – keep reminding yourself that it will pass.

- Have lots of loo roll at the ready (splash out and buy the quilted stuff!)

- Try to do quiet things, that distract you or your child from any stomach pain or discomfort. Reading helped me. I love reading - I have read about three hundred books in my life, add or subtract fifty. I am usually in trouble for reading all night so at the beginning of the diet it was good to be able to lie and read without having the electric light turned off.

- If you try to control any spinning or flapping usually, then go on – indulge yourself! Mind you, I wouldn't suggest this if you are at school or work.

- Have some calming music and lights in your room. I love lava lamps and coloured lights; my room is full of them.

- Indulge your obsessions. Surround yourself with information about your favourite topic and absorb yourself in it. Mine is making websites and computers in general. I played on the Playstation for days – pure bliss!

Tips for parents of AD/HD kids

- Really energetic kids get even more hyper when they have the gluten and casein taken out of their system, I would say that doing loads of physical exercise would help. Joe was really wild and bounced all over the place and I am sure if he could have been taken somewhere to use up some of that aggression and energy it would have been easier for him. (And therefore for us too.)

- Play wild games, like twister and just join in with them and be generally mad.

- Same applies as with smaller kids – if you don't want something broken, remove it. Joe destroys most things. Mum let him rip paper to his heart's contents. We had a competition to see who could rip up the most pages of the telephone directory. Joe is into ripping up paper.

- Mum bought Joe one of those stretchy figures that you can pull the arms and legs about and twist into any shape you like, thinking it would help to get rid of stress. Within an hour he had managed to gouge a great big hole in it and gooey stuff got everywhere. Don't bother with those stress balls and things. Joe can wreck one in an instant!

All in all, I would say that my biggest tip of all is – remember that this is very positive and it will pass!

6

Getting into the Diet –
the Fog Begins to Lift

And now the good bit: the storm passes

I would think most of you will be breathing a sigh of relief at the prospect of a good bit. Believe me, the storm does pass and all the withdrawals become worthwhile. This is the bit that you have been waiting for!

It took a week or maybe ten days for Ben and a bit less for Joe to go through the worst of the withdrawals. For me it took a little longer, though my withdrawal symptoms were never so severe as theirs. After all, I am not as severe as them (a little bit of sarcasm there!). Seriously though, I think that that was because I had had twelve years of gluten in my system.

The stomach pains began to subside for all of us and, sorry to be disgusting and I will try to word it as best I can, but Joe and I began to poo normally for the first time in our lives. Still on the poo topic, Ben continued to poo on his own without the help of enemas and laxatives. To this day he has never needed any help since he began the diet.

Both Joe's and my bloated stomachs flattened too. That was very strange to see when they had been like that for as long as I can remember.

Now here is something else that was very strange at this time.

As I may have said, I am the kind of person who avoids crowds and noise and likes to be still and on my own, but at this time I felt very energetic and spent a lot of time on the trampoline with my sisters. The tiredness and the lethargy that I felt were replaced by this tremendous surge of energy and I felt like I was 'walking on air' (now I finally know what this expression means). I ran about everywhere, testing out this new burst of energy. All this was very unlike me as I am usually a very sedate person, preferring my own company and the company of computers and books.

This is one thing that is pretty cool about this diet. Joe, who is so hyperactive and energetic and pretty much the opposite of me in that way, reacted in a completely different way to me. Straight after the withdrawals I had this mad energy burst, whereas Joe changed and was very pale and still and definitely too quiet. The diet seemed to swap us around.

Ben went from being totally spaced out to being very alert and noticing everyone around him. Mum says he 'landed back on this planet' (he always was, but this is Mum's expression and maybe other parents will understand what she means).

Here is one thing that was so amazing. Ben did a full head banging session all day and all night for four days and then he started to talk! He suddenly said 'I wah bwe pwee' and 'I wah toe pwee'. That was Ben talk for 'I want bread please' and 'I want toast please' (which wasn't exactly a good thing to say, as we had no gluten-free bread at the time).

Another thing that happened was he stopped this hysterical laughing completely. We kind of missed it as we were all so used to it and he was so funny, but I do realise that no one could go through life laughing crazily to themselves.

I must admit that the one thing that didn't pass for ages and that you need to know about this diet is that you feel very hungry. There seemed to be a black hole where my stomach should be, which sucked up everything except my hunger, and however much food I put in it, it didn't seem to make any difference.

The only solution to that one is to make sure that the meals are filling and there are plenty of snacks around. Have a go at GF/CF baking and get other members of the family to help. It can be fun.

The diet is healthier than the usual junk foods that we used to eat, so there is no need to worry about snacking more often. After all, you are not likely to be stuffing your or your child's face with cream cakes and sweets any more (although it does sound a tempting idea).

As I have said before, my bad breath got much better and the black rings around my eyes started to fade, but took months to go completely.

For those of you with AS, here's something that you should know. Asperger-wise I didn't feel very much different for quite some time. I would say over two months, at least. I was very disappointed about that. I had this idea that I would suddenly become popular and outgoing. I guess I was expecting a total personality change. That still hasn't happened and never will, of course, but I am quite happy and accepting of who I am now. I feel more at ease with myself and happy with my life than ever before. To me that is the most positive thing about this diet.

Mum says that I am not so wooden (I never was obviously, but I believe it meant that I stood as if I was made of wood) and I apparently have a much better sense of humour but obviously I cannot comment on those kinds of things.

Don't get me wrong; I am not 'cured' and certainly wouldn't want to be. In fact my main grievance when I first heard of the diet was that it was devised to 'cure' AS and autistic people and I was quite offended. But I now realise that I am what I am but there are some bits of autism or AS that are certainly not desirable.

Mum says that if there was only one benefit for each one of us, she would have continued to keep us GF/CF. I am glad that is not the way it is and there are so many benefits for all of us.

Routine and change

Another little tip here for parents. My brother likes to do something the same each time and gets really stressed or weird if he can't do that. If he has sat in one chair, or done something even once, then he expects that that is how it is to be done every time.

On a Saturday we go to a disabled sports session at Blackpool sports centre called Blackpool Bears. Here all ages and abilities can mess around and participate in many different sports to whatever level they like. There is a dinner break and we all go upstairs and eat our packed lunch. Each week Ben insists that we sit in exactly the same place on the floor and goes mad if anyone else is sat there.

Maybe kids who are picky eaters have things like that bothering them. You really need to stop and think of things through the eyes of the autistic person to find out what is bothering them.

Autistic kids like routine but even if this is not obvious and they don't have a massive tantrum, they could still react to things not being quite the same by refusing to eat. This is just my thought on the subject.

Here are some ways the diet changed my and my brothers' senses. (Maybe now we are more sensible! Get it?)

Sound sensitivities

> "Now I have a good diet where no one shouts at me as much and there's no more bells in my ears and I haven't got tummy ache and Mum's cooking isn't minging any more"
>
> *–Joe Jackson*

One problem that I have had all my life is that my ears are really sensitive. When I was younger I used to scream and go mad when we went to parties and stuff like that. I don't know what people used to make of it, but I do remember that everything that other kids liked to do always seem so loud and often distorted. It was like that dreadful echoing in a swimming pool. I never did learn to swim properly and most of that was due to the fact that the noise disorientated me and made me feel scared.

Apparently, there is a difference between 'foreground' and 'background noise'. People with AS or autism have difficulties 'tuning out' background noise but, though I still have to try hard, I can now tell much better when someone is talking directly to me. It is as if the diet has syringed away the bits that were blocked up and plugged up the bits that were too sensitive (this, of course isn't what happened literally but I do think that it is quite an accurate analogy).

I do think Joe still has difficulty with tuning out background noise. His listening is still bad and people should be aware that the diet helps different people in different ways. Joe had some kind of ringing in his ears and he says this has gone, though I have to admit I never do know what is 'Joetalk'. He makes up the most bizarre things sometimes.

Ben is still very sound sensitive and often covers his ears but nowhere near as much as before the diet. This is one of the most noticeable improvements with him. He now sticks his fingers in his ears when he goes into a new place or when a new television programme or computer programme is starting. It is as if he thinks it is going to hurt his ears but then he realises that it doesn't. This is a really big bonus for Ben, particularly because when someone spends their life with their fingers in their ears, they can't do anything else with their hands. I always wondered if he would ever learn to write because of this. He hasn't yet, of course, but I presume he will one day. Having his fingers in his ears is the first thing you notice about him when he has had an infringement (more about that later).

A lot of kids with autism make 'weird' noises and squeak and squeal and blow raspberries and stuff like that. They shut their eyes too, particularly when people come near them. I reckon that all this is to block other people and the rest of the world out. To be honest I kind of envy them. I know that I couldn't do those kinds of things, and it just isn't conducive to living in this world, but still, when people are 'in your face' or things are just too confusing, it would be nice to shut things out like that.

Ben does still squeal and shout and sing really loud and make noises for no apparent reason, but he is only just learning to talk now and maybe if his ears were messed up somehow he is now experimenting with new sounds. Not many people can understand him yet but he is trying. Maybe one day he'll tell us about these things himself.

Eye contact and facial expressions

> "Bad foods change me and hurt my tummy but I like them
> and still pinch them. I have changed now and when I am
> changed I can read everyone's love and love is my best
> teacher. I am asking God to keep me like this and help other
> children who want to eat bad foods."
>
> *–Joe Jackson*

Something else that Ben does is covering his ears when the lights
are too bright. I think all of his senses get muddled up and he
doesn't know what is bothering him.

These are things that the diet makes much more bearable.

So many people say that their child has better eye contact; I
have read that on the Internet a lot. Adults seem to make a real big
deal out of eye contact. Mum often says to me 'Luke, I am over
here, not over there' or 'Look at me when I am talking to you'. It's
as if people think that if you don't look at them, then you can't
hear them. This is just not logical.

Ben went through a phase where no one was allowed to look at
him or he would scream 'no' or growl. We had to sit in the car and
look down at the floor or with our heads to the side. We have a
Toyota Lucida Previa with eight seats and the seats face each other.
This is a real pain when Ben is like this. We used to get shouted at
all the time just for looking at Ben! Mum spent months saying
'looking' and pointing to people's eyes to explain what they were
doing and that it was OK. Since the diet that has all changed and
comes back again only after an infringement.

I think the reason some children have better eye contact with
the diet is that all of their over-sensitivities have lessened. If all
your senses are too strong, then people's eyes bore into you and
the lights burn your eyes and the noises and smells are all too con-

fusing. Now I am not saying that I am like that in every way but I do understand.

At the Blackpool Bears I watch autistic people there covering their ears or their eyes and I want to go and scream at their parents and tell them to at least give the diet a decent try. It may not help, I am sure that it doesn't help everyone, but no one knows until they try.

Joe says he can 'read people's faces' and though I am sure it is not in the same way, I kind of know what he means. Joe wrote on a magnetic board thing the other day and gave it to Mum. It said 'you are unhappy' (we had all made a mess as usual). He seemed really pleased that he knew this. Joe is much more sensitive to people's feelings than I am.

I think Ben will be more like me. At the moment, if someone cries then Ben laughs and if he is being shouted at (though this doesn't happen often enough in my opinion) he laughs really hard. He is a very strange boy, but so much fun.

I am never sure what expressions I have on my face but I can tell that other people are meaning something without speaking now. I don't remember ever being able to do that before (and Mum says she notices this). One example of this is my Mum pulls a really strange face and raises her eyebrows then tells an outright lie. This is usually in front of my brothers when she doesn't want them to know something. She will say 'It was really boring in town wasn't it Luke' and pull a really strange face and I now know that I have to nod and agree so Joe doesn't start moaning and saying he wishes he could have gone. A bit deceitful I reckon, but hey, these things have to be done!

Textures and sensitivities

I know lots of autistic kids naturally restrict what they eat and this must be pretty hard for their parents. I think that that is a lot to do with the textures, smells and looks of a meal or food. I know that it must take a bit more thinking about, but if you realise that your child doesn't like sloppy food, then maybe you could add something to it to make it crunchy, or make a batter, or coat it in breadcrumbs or cornflakes (GF/CF of course). Mum does that quite often in our house.

I have always hated getting my hands sticky or dirty and hate the feeling of sand, cotton wool balls and the feel of polystyrene and stuff like that.

I certainly haven't suddenly started to wallow in mud or bury myself in the sand but I can tolerate messy things more than I used to be able to. We went to the sand hills two weeks ago and after a while I got off the concrete slope where I usually stay and started to mess around in the sand. I would never have done anything like that before. The warm stuff actually felt quite nice, though not the wet sand.

Maybe some would say I have just grown up but it is funny that both Ben and I had the same problem and got over it when we went on this diet.

Ben is obviously the same as me with this kind of stuff but a lot, lot worse. He used to spit and scream and refuse to go near paints, messy stuff, sand or anything like that. He now touches some textures that he wouldn't before and he will dig in a sand pit with a spade or paint with a paintbrush. He still doesn't like getting his hands messy but doesn't go anywhere near as mad now. He just gets someone to wipe off every minute bit.

Ben refused to wear any clothes at all pre diet. Mum would wrestle with him for ages just to get a vest on him and as soon as we turned our back he had stripped again. He is much better with that now apart from certain things. In fact he has gone the other way and won't take them off. Sometimes he is just plain awkward!

Ben also used to spend loads of time getting Mum or anyone to squeeze his feet and stick their fingers really hard into his eyes. He obviously needed this feeling and he doesn't do that anymore unless he is very tired or has had an infringement.

Taste and smell

This is one thing that for me has changed quite a lot. There are so many smells that I really can't stand to the point that I would keep away from them at all costs. The main thing I can think of here is going into a market. When there is the smell of fish, perfume and all sorts mixed together I felt as if I was going to explode and be sick.

We get our fruit from our local market now and all that kind of stuff doesn't bother me at all anymore.

I know that Ben's taste has changed too. Ben wouldn't eat pasta before the diet. I presume it was too slimy. He now eats gluten free pasta and foods with that kind of texture with no problem. He still won't eat mixed up textures and quite a few things, but the problems with his senses are Ben's biggest problem so I reckon that he is doing pretty well.

After a while, these are the kinds of things that you forget were ever a problem and that's why I thought it was important to write them down. It is only after an infringement when something returns that all the bad bits come flooding back (quite literally).

I think it is pretty cool just how many things this diet helps.

7

Accidents Will Happen!
Watch Out for Icebergs

"If I steal stuff like a biscuit I get really bad tummy ache but I feel really mean sometimes and sometimes really silly and I can't stop it and can't stop being angry sometimes too."

—Joe Jackson

Since we began this diet there have been quite a few little 'slip-ups'. It is pretty impossible to escape from getting some off limit foods at least once or twice. Maybe you or your child will do it on purpose and give in to the craving – I know I have, and more than once, too – and maybe it will be accidental.

When you are well into the diet you will know exactly when your child has had something they shouldn't. The signs to look for are a general regression and the same kind of signs as pre-diet. Here are some:

- Red ears – often only one

- A change in behaviour – more clinging on to someone or more detached

- An increase in autistic behaviour such as hand flapping or lining up and dragging people around (Ben does this loads when he's had something he shouldn't)
- Less eye contact
- Hysterical laughing
- Aggression
- Hyperactivity
- Bad temperedness
- Changes in pooing habits (sorry, there I go again!)
- Changes in sleep habits

Obviously if it is you yourself that it is doing the diet, then you are likely to know whether you have had any infringements. However, if you start to feel bad and have a churning stomach or diarrhoea or lose concentration more easily, then you should look carefully at everything you are eating and see if some malt extract, or gluten crumbs or casein, is getting into your diet without your realising it.

If there is still a problem with you or your child, then maybe you should explore other issues such as phenols and candida. I have written a little about other intolerances and other problems later in the book and obviously there are links at the back where you can find out more.

Either way it is impossible to say exactly what will happen and what the reaction will be like. It is also impossible to say how long it will last or how severe it will be. I think those kinds of things vary from person to person. I think that saying how someone will react is a bit like trying to work out how someone will react to a bad situation. Some people get angry, some people cry, some people withdraw into themselves and some people just feel bad inside but put on a brave outward face.

Ben reacts badly to aspartame and has screaming tantrums and I get really bad headaches when I've had monosodium glutamate. Joe goes completely haywire when he has had these or colourings.

Remember the black rings around the eyes come back very easily and that these take ages to go. If they appear again there is a need to look for an infringement as this is almost always what causes it (sometimes you or your child may have raided the cupboard – I have to admit, I did!).

Once, when Mum was making herself a sandwich, Ben came in and was pestering her for something to eat (or his seventeenth meal, to be more accurate!). She made him a rice cake and jam and then absentmindedly handed the sandwich to Ben and started to eat the rice cake herself! The last time Ben ate bread he was in the bathroom so now whenever he gets something off limit he rushes into the bathroom and eats it there, because he thinks that is the only place he is allowed to eat gluten food.

Also, one time when we were going to have Sunday dinner and it was all sorted out and then, after we had eaten it, we found out that it had Bisto in (that contains wheat starch). We felt ill for about a week. Joe and I were both off school and it was torture.

It was soon apparent that we react a lot worse when we eat 'bad foods' now than when we first started the diet. That's why you have to be so careful, one slip-up and it costs you about a week of pain.

I often get 'panic attacks' in crowds and these seem to increase when I have had an infringement. All react differently: Joe's can be seen immediately – he is completely hyper and turns really spiteful. I feel terrible immediately; I have stomach pains and a churning feeling. I have learnt, though, to recognise when I am eating different foods. Aspartame makes me feel sick, lactose and casein give me a funny burning feeling at the back of my throat, gluten gives me stomach ache and monosodium glutomate gives me a very bad headache. Ben only seems to be more 'weird' after a while (though I don't really know what he feels like; he doesn't tend to let on that he has a headache or a stomach-ache – this may sound stupid but some people can do that without talking, Ben doesn't)

Ben isn't like me and Joe in his reactions. Nothing really obvious happens with gluten and casein until the day after when it has the effect of heroin; it makes him feel 'spaced out' and he keeps closing his eyes and laughing hysterically. In this state, to him no one else seems to exist; you could scream into his ear and he wouldn't take any notice.

With aspartame and monosodium glutamate, he reacts really badly and gets as bad tempered as – well as Ben when he is bad tempered (I cannot think of an appropriate simile). He lies around on the floor screaming and kicking and throws things everywhere. In fact he is really quite horrible.

I have said before that I go to a disabled sports session called Blackpool Bears, though I do think it is strange to think of AS as a disability. I have a far higher spelling and reading age than loads of other people at my school but yet I am considered 'disabled'. I think that the only disabling thing in this world is people's inability to accept difference. The disabling bits of AS for me were the stomach pain and the sound sensitivity and the diet has helped those.

In Blackpool Sports Centre there is a bar there which, when Blackpool Bears is on, is usually absolutely seething with people. The first time I went in to the bar to buy some chips and a cup of coffee for Mum, I just stared at all the people there (there seemed to be millions of them, and duplicating by the second) and had what I now know as a 'panic attack'. I just started to cry to myself and got all, well, panicky inside. I was still shaking about half an hour later. It is hard to breathe and I can't help but wring my hands and flap them about when I feel like that. I know I bug my sisters and embarrass them, but I really can't help it.

I have been trying to link these attacks to infringements and there does seem to be a connection. I still do go all shaky in games – I don't really know why this is – and I have found the best solution is reading. When I say reading I don't mean just sit down with a book every time you get nervous, I simply mean that you should try to read anything that comes to hand. It really helps; I have never had a panic attack once in games, though I have come very close.

I have not done nutrition in too much detail at school, but there is enough stuff on adverts to let you know that a 'balanced' diet is what is important. It doesn't take too much working out for yourself, then, to know whether you are getting adequate nutrition. If you only eat one or two foods, there is a pretty good chance that there is something missing. A dietician may help, but here is a word of warning. Even if you are lucky and have a good dietician who believes that this diet really does help and who is encouraging, there can still be problems. Most dieticians give the same advice as they give to people with coeliac disease, but for some reason these people can eat very small amounts of gluten without it affecting them. I know this from first hand experience.

My Mum has had Joe on a GF/CF diet for years but as she got desperate when his hyperactivity was really at its worse, she contacted Marilyn Le Breton on the AiA help line. Marilyn told her that the malt extract in rice crispies would probably be affecting Joe. Mum stopped him having them the day after. Anyway, he came home from school in a really bad mood and wandered about saying 'I REALLY feel like some rice crispies, I keep thinking about them all the time'. I think that was pretty cool, to get such strong evidence that he was addicted to them.

After a few mad days, he really calmed down and has never been quiet like he was then. He still is very hyper and fidgety and talks too much and is never still, but nothing like he was before this new diet.

8

A Few Added Extras – Sailing into Foreign Ports!

"My tummy is still not good because now I am having no sugar for a little bit. I have been on a special diet for a long time now but since doing a proper one I am not shouted at so much and I can read and write better. I can't have milk, eggs which make me get spots all over and I can't breath, and gluten and sesame and loads of things but Mum can still cook really good food and now I am not pooing all my muscles out so I can do press ups."

–Joe Jackson

Other intolerances

I have saved this bit till last because some people are lucky enough to be fine with only the GF/CF diet. Some people, though, have other intolerances as well. It is important to say, though, that these are not evident after only a week or two. Mum gets loads of phone calls from parents asking if their child is reacting to something else because their behaviour has really worsened. The withdrawals do take a long time to finish completely. You need to be on the GF/CF diet alone for a good few weeks, maybe months, before you can safely say that you or your child may be reacting to something else. That was what happened to us.

Please remember that I am only twelve and don't know all that there is to know about this kind of stuff but I will tell you what I know and you can look at the back of the book, for further reading.

It is recommended, again by Paul Shattock, that, once the gluten and casein is out of the system and there is a suspicion that something is affecting someone, they take the food that they seem to like the most out of the diet and see if there are any changes. He suggests doing that for ten to fourteen days. After that put it back again and see if there is a change in the person for the worse. Some people are intolerant to corn and soya and other things too. It depends on the individual. Joe reacts badly to eggs and sesame and lots more things than Ben and me.

This gets really confusing for friends and family, I must say. We go to Grandad's house and we are allowed bananas, then we are not, then we are again. It then happens all over again with something else. Poor Grandad never does know what to give us.

In all food and other things there are chemicals called phenols. Many people on the autistic spectrum have problems processing them so they build up in their bodies and cause more strange behaviours. This is called the sulphation process and seems to be the bit that Joe has big problems with. To help this process Mum puts Epsom salts in the bath and whatever it is, it is absorbed through the skin.

This is where the diet gets beyond me and you really must go to the links at the back of the book.

Candida

About three months into the diet Joe, Ben and I were all feeling ill, although we were sure we hadn't had an infringement. As I have said, one of the physical signs that someone is addicted to gluten or casein is red ears. In a lot of cases, just one red ear. Well Ben had bright red cheeks and two red ears. His cheeks looked as if he had been put in front of a heater and left there. After a while on the GF/CF diet, his behaviour had changed a lot and he had stopped most of the laughing, but his cheeks were still scarlet. He had also developed patches of sore, dry skin around his chin and his mouth. Nothing seemed to get rid of them and Mum can't put cream on Ben anyway because he hates anything sticky or slimy and would spit and choke as soon as the cream came near him.

Joe also had a really sore mouth.

It looked as if he had two sets of lips, one above the top lip and one below the bottom. It cracked and bled and caused him real problems. It was these things that made Mum search again for answers.

I had a churning stomach and diarrhoea on and off and Joe was the same.

Marilyn Le Breton mentioned to Mum that some people have a problem with candida and there is research going on to show that it stays in the gut, particularly of people on the autistic spectrum. We had all had thrush on and off all of our lives, and been on anti-biotics a lot too. All this pointed to the idea that we may have had candida. Our GP apparently had heard of this theory and has been pretty good about the diet, so he prescribed us all Nystatin. That was what helped to kill off the candida. Candida is a fungus that grows and feeds off yeast and sugar so we had to go on a low sugar and yeast diet.

This was particularly hard, especially as we were already well into the diet. I never realised how hard it was to cut out gluten, yeast, sugar, casein, aspartame, eggs and monosodium glutomate!

When we started the diet I was expecting it only to last for about three days and to be completely painless.

How wrong I was.

About two days later, I suddenly had this humungous craving for sugar. I asked Mum about this and if we could now go back to eating sugary stuff and that was when I learned – shock, horror – that I had to go on this diet for about two weeks, maybe more!

Also, it turned out that when you start the candida die off (that is what it is called) you have a mad craving for sugar and yeast; this was the candida craving food.

If you or your child ever get candida, then my advice is to make a temporary store of sugar free and yeast free foods, put them in a box or something, then lock all the other cupboards. Sadly, we didn't take that advice.

I was craving so much that I managed to get hold of some icing and peanut butter and sneak it into my room. Mum soon found out, though, and it was back to being even stricter with the Nystatin and the low sugar.

Joe was a lot more hyperactive than usual (not to mention destructive and annoying) and Ben went back to head-banging the kitchen door, which we had seen so many times when we first started the GF/CF diet. He then just kind of ignored everyone completely and seemed really nervy and scared all the time. He is the kind of child that goes very quiet and scared when he is faced with stuff he is unsure of, but is never like that at home.

At this time, he went very pale and needed nappy change after nappy change. When we reduced our sugar to none at all, Mum used 32 nappies in about two hours. He had such a sore backside.

I felt absolutely horrible; my stomach felt like a vast black hole, which consumed everything in reach except my hunger. It kept churning and gurgling; it felt like I was constantly being tossed around on a rough sea.

After a couple of weeks of low sugar and low yeast, Joe's and Ben's faces were still the same and Ben developed thrush (I won't mention where!). It seemed the candida was still being fed and we had to cut out all sugar and all yeast, not just some. Was that a bad time! I couldn't sleep for thinking about sugar, not that I can sleep anyway, but all the time I was just trying to fight back the urge to find a way, any way to get something sweet.

Joe was just the same. He kept getting out of his room in the night and trying to find the key to the kitchen door. Ben was doing the head banging bit with a vengeance and it all got too much. We just couldn't do it and after a week, Mum let us have fruit spreads with no added sugar, on rice or corn cakes. That seemed to do the trick and satisfy the urges.

The Feingold diet

Joe was at that time, and still is, on the Feingold diet, which was where he had to cut out artificial colourings and nitrates and that. The Feingold diet is for hyperactive kids and the GF/CF diet is for AS and autistic kids. It seems that Joe is a bit of a mix of everything. Some bits of him are so like me and Ben and other bits of him are so different. That is the beauty of a big family I suppose.

9

Frequently Asked Questions

I am sure that as you contemplate taking gluten, casein, monosodium glutamate and aspartame out of your or your child's diet, there must be loads of questions in your mind. I have attempted to think of some that you are likely to ask and to give the answers as best as I can although these are only my answers based on personal experience and, as I have said before, I am only twelve.

The questions can apply to someone doing the diet for themselves or to parents who are doing it with their child.

I have just received the Sunderland urine analysis and it shows no gluten/casein peak or a very small one. Does that mean the diet will not work?

No, it does not necessarily mean that the diet will not work. It is always worth a go as it may have an effect even if there is no gluten/casein peak on the results.

My child eats very little already. I am worried about them losing weight.

Lots of children restrict the kinds of foods that they eat and if they are only eating gluten and casein foods then it is a very good sign. There is a very good chance that the diet will have a positive effect. (I have tried to give some thoughts and hints on this topic, in an earlier chapter.)

I am worried about the withdrawals. Will it be too much to take?

No two people are alike and the withdrawals may be severe or may be mild. Whatever you or your children are experiencing, remember that it is positive. I have given some tips on how to cope in an earlier chapter.

Can we go off the diet just once in a while?

NO – you will be giving a quick fix to yourself or your child. The diet needs to be stuck to rigidly otherwise it is not worth doing.

Is the diet affordable? The food seems so expensive.

It is quite expensive, but it is worth it. If you have a good GP and can convince them that the diet needs doing, lots of foods can be got on prescription so that cuts down the cost by a lot. There is an appendix listing the recommended prescriptible foods.

I have just had a 'slip up'. Does that mean that I will have to go through the withdrawals again?

An infringement will cause different reactions in different people. (I have written a lot about that earlier in the book.) Because there will be only a small amount of gluten or casein in the system, it will take a lot less time to get rid of it – nothing like a full withdrawal. As I have said before, though, no two people react the same.

Is it possible to eat out occasionally and still do the diet?

If it is, then we haven't found many places yet! Sorry, I know that is not the answer you wanted and I suppose if you phoned up a place in advance they might cater for you or let you take your own food but…even chips can be risky, as the fat they are cooked in may have had something in it that contained gluten and this would contaminate the chips. MacDonald's and Burger King's French fries are OK as long as nothing else has been cooked in the fat that week. The burgers are cooked separately and MacDonald's Hash Browns are all GF/CF.

Does all the family have to do the diet? My other children really don't want to.

In an ideal world, it is better if the person doing the diet has no temptation and there is nothing in the house that could possibly contaminate their food…however, as long as the kitchen is organised so that there are strict GF/CF areas and everyone is careful, it is possible for people who don't need the GF/CF diet to eat 'ordinary' food. We do that in our house though the main meal is always GF/CF for all of us.

There seems to be so much taken out of this diet. Do I need to take supplements? I am especially concerned about calcium.

You can take or give your child a multi vitamin supplement but if the diet is balanced there should be all that is needed in the food. It depends on the individual and what they eat. There are calcium enriched Soya milks and products. A dietician will give more advice on this if you are worried.

Do I have to stay on this diet forever or will I be able to go back to 'normal' foods?

I would not think about going back onto gluten and casein foods. It becomes a way of life very quickly. All individuals are different and I can only give my opinion and I would say that if the gluten and casein have done the harm in the first place, then stick with the diet and don't go off it. Obviously if someone has given it a decent try for a year or so and there is really no difference at all then it is up to you whether to give up.

Can I buy GF/CF foods in ordinary supermarkets or do I have to go to specialist shops.

Most supermarkets have an organic range and they are increasing. Health shops will have anything that you can't get. The basics can be got in supermarkets, though.

Epilogue

Well there you have it – a brief outline of the journey through the GF/CF diet! At the risk of becoming a bore (though I am sure many would already say I am) I hope this book has helped you to understand your child that little bit more if they are already on the diet, or has succeeded in encouraging you to take that first step for either yourself or your child. Whatever place you are at in your GF/CF journey, either taking that first step or refining your child's diet, down to as 'clean' (Mum's word) as possible, by dealing with salicylates, phenols, candida, artificial colourings and additives, nitrates and addressing the whole sulphation problem, I would like to think that I have been informative and encouraging. That has been my aim. As I have said before, I do try to be helpful.

I have deliberately mentioned all these more complicated bits which I have touched upon in my previous chapter, to help you to realise that there is always a next step and a little bit more you can do to move on in your journey. Personally I think this very 'advanced' diet is for extremely sensitive autistic people and people with AD/HD but of course I can only speak from experience within my family and my observations of the people I meet and talk to.

For both parents of children anywhere on the autistic spectrum, including children with AD/HD, and for people on the spectrum themselves, I really hope that you give this diet a go and it takes you or your child to the place where you want to be. If not, then at least you can say you have given it your best shot and that's all anyone can do – try their best.

One final word – once having embarked on your GF/CF journey, just don't abandon ship, and keep scrubbing those decks. Sorry to sound corny, but I just couldn't resist!

Appendices

1

Implementing the diet – A word from Mum

It is not easy to be considered a 'crank'. It is not easy to know, in your heart and soul, the importance of this diet, to have the proof smiling up at you each day but yet not be able to give scientific evidence to the medical profession. It is not easy to be frowned upon and looked upon with suspicion for doing the best for your children. It is not easy to be made to feel guilty for 'depriving' your children of the only foods they enjoy, when they already 'have enough to deal with'.

These are the things I find difficult; these are the things I would like to change.

As for actually implementing the diet, believe me when I say that it really is not difficult.

I am sure that even after reading Luke's first hand account of the benefits, there are still those of you who are considering this far too difficult. All I can say to that is that if I can do it then anyone can. I am not superwoman!

People often ask how I cope with having so many children. In fact there seems to be a stock set of responses when anyone first discovers how many children I have. 'Goodness how do you cope, I find it difficult with only two' or 'didn't you have a television!' This actually gets a bit wearing and when they discover the boys have special needs, my halo starts hovering above my head.

Actually all my children have special needs; all children have special needs. The girls and Matthew constantly have to deal with living in a house that resembles a fortress, with the embarrassment of Ben wandering around naked when their friends are here or licking everything in sight when we go out. We cannot go to parties as a family, because the boys dislike crowds and loud noise and we cannot eat out often because of the diet. Along with dealing with puberty, life in general, schoolwork and all that life throws a young person, these are added burdens for any sibling of a child on the autistic spectrum and ones that most of you, I'm sure, are familiar with. These, too, are the difficult things; these are the things I would like to change.

So how do I manage this diet and negotiate seven children?

My childhood gave me a head start I suppose. Growing up with my sister has stood me in good stead for living with my kids and dealing with all their intolerances. Heather has multiple, severe, life threatening allergies. Issues such as cross contamination therefore become second nature to me. I grew up in a household where I couldn't use the same towel if I had touched an egg or something else that she would react to. I must say I did 'test her out' once to see if it was psychosomatic. That really was a scary time and I certainly only did it once. Here's a public apology, Heather!

I became quite adept at adapting a recipe to suit Heather when I was doing my O level cookery many moons ago, though I must say that not a lot was edible then. My Dad was kind enough to suffer many a torturous meal prepared by me. I have come a long way since then.

I think in some ways, though, such severe allergies are easier for everyone to understand. The subtle (though not so subtle in many children) changes and effects that gluten and casein have are a lot harder for those around to accept.

After much heartache, trauma and suspicion, Joe responded well to the implementation of this diet when he was very young. Before that he was quite literally wasting away, suffering seemingly inexplicable vomiting and diarrhoea. That was one of the most frightening times of my life and if I am able to prevent even one person going through that trauma, then this will have been worthwhile.

The reason I write of this is that everyone will have their own reason for wanting to embark on this diet or implement it with their child. For Joe it really was a medical necessity and the removal of malt extract, monosodium glutamate and aspartame along with following the Feingold diet, and killing off the candida, were the keys to the changes in his behaviour.

For Ben, amelioration of chronic constipation was enough indeed for me to pursue this diet, but the massive changes in awareness, behaviour and language outreached all my expectations.

For some of you there may be certain parts of your AS that you find debilitating whilst many of you will be seeking any way to help your child maximise their full potential. As parents, that is what we all strive for.

Whatever your reasons, I hope that in some way I can encourage you to take the plunge if you are still wavering, and embark on the journey of the GF/CF diet.

I am not now going to repeat what Luke has already said, nor spell out the fine details of how to implement this diet. There are books that do that far more succinctly than I could ever do in one chapter. I will however, tell you how I manage in the hope that you will realise that it can be done.

My family, and my sister in particular, will be laughing at this section. It is a standing joke that I am the first to beg any leftovers from family gatherings and woe betide anyone who throws away any unfinished food. I am an expert at making meals out of leftovers!

It's not that I dislike cooking or that I can't do it. Just that having to cook and prepare for seven children, every day without exception, gets to be a real bind – especially when the children resemble a swarm of locusts!

I am sure those of you with children with multiple allergies or intolerances or following the Feingold and the GF/CF diet, will agree with me that to be purely GF/CF is a breeze once you modify your way of life.

My first and most valuable tip for those of you starting out on this is don't panic. This really isn't difficult. This diet is all about getting back to basics. Meat, vegetables and fruit are all part of a balanced diet. None of them contain gluten or casein. Eggs are a valuable source of protein and omelettes made with a splash of milk substitute and a tasty filling of chopped ham and tomatoes make a substantial breakfast or snack.

This diet really is about revising the way we think. Who was it that said that breakfast consisted of toast and cereal? Who told us that we have roast dinners on Sunday? If your child will eat it and you can buy it or bake it, then stick with it. My children often have left over macaroni 'cheese' for breakfast or cereal for supper.

I am a morning person. When I was doing my degree I studied in the morning and now I bake in the morning. The boys wake up extremely early so if I am out of bread or something for packed lunches, then that is my time to switch on the oven and make up a quick mix. Now don't imagine that I am there kneading bread in the early hours of the morning. When I say I make their bread, that really does consist of nothing more than throwing water into the mix and putting the mix into a tin and leaving it to cook. I get my bread mix on prescription and the same with the cake mix. It really is very easy and if you or your child likes the ready-made breads, then even better, because those too can be obtained on prescription.

Many of you will recoil in horror at the thought of getting up early to bake. You will find your own times and your own level and many of you may prefer not to bake at all.

I have a large double oven and tend to have a cooking day when I make lasagnes, shepherds pies, stews and casseroles en masse and then freeze them. The same is true for baking, although these never get a chance to be frozen as I am usually knocked over in the stampede as soon as the oven door is opened.

If anyone would have told me a year ago that I would be baking cakes and bread I would have laughed. As I am sure is the case for many of you, I have very little time to spend on cooking. I have Ben with me twenty-four hours a day and he can never be left unsupervised. That gives an indication of the amount of cooking time needed and I hope will give you confidence to realise that you too can do this.

One thing, which I suppose is particular to me, is that I tend to do things in phases. I tend to have a cooking or baking spree and the kids feel as if their birthdays and Christmas have all come rolled into one, as I laden the house with all sorts of goodies – then I get bored! I then have a gardening fit or go on a cleaning spree or simply sit and mess with my computer. At these time I usually have lasagnes, shepherds pies and fruit crumbles in the freezer from when I was particularly virtuous, so I simply throw them in the oven and at the children and get back to what I am doing.

I have learnt not to feel guilty if I throw peanut butter rice cakes or a quick baked potato or a bowl of beans at the children whilst I do my own thing. I soon get back to my cooking phase and stock up again. All of us have our own ways of coping and these are mine.

2

Recipes

Many of us with children on this diet end up getting quite excited about new kitchen appliances that enable us to make our own GF/CF products (how sad is that!).

Two things that I find indispensable are my yoghurt maker and my waffle maker but I am sure each of you will soon find your own ways of making life easier whilst producing foods that all the family can eat.

This is not a recipe book – there are some excellent ones available (see Further Reading). However, I have included some recipes in the hope that you will realise just how quick and easy GF/CF cooking can be. Most of the recipes for the main meals can be pre-prepared or just thrown in a wok or pan and cooked and served quickly. Many of the ingredient lists look quite lengthy but that is purely to give an idea of what can be used. I tend to throw in allowed herbs and spices as I cook. The quantities in the recipes are to suit an average family, so obviously I double or treble the amounts. Those of you with a family like mine should do the same. I have included quite a few 'grown up' meals as most of my children like to try new things and to eat spicy foods. At those times I simply do something which is tried and tested, for Ben. When I find something he will eat I tend to make larger quantities and freeze Ben-size portions for the times when the rest are having adventurous meals.

Obviously, for those of you with added intolerances, on the Feingold diet, removing phenols or salicylates, or on the candida diet, you can miss out or substitute the offending foods.

My apologies for the variations in measurements. For baking I use American cups and spoons, and to be honest, to get these recipes written down for the book, I painstakingly weighed out everything else as I cooked. I normally just throw things in and most things seem to turn out fine. This section has taken me longer to write than it took Luke to write the whole book, so I hope it is of help to some of you.

There is a section later which lists many suppliers of GF/CF ingredients. Many Chinese supermarkets also stock these. I personally use flours and xanthan gum from Barbara's Kitchen.

Bread, cakes and biscuits

This section should really be written by my daughter Anna. She is enthusiastically wading her way through many a GF/CF recipe and, as far as baking is concerned, I am slowly becoming redundant. Starting out with the baking was the hardest part for me as all recipes seemed to call for eggs and Joe and Ben are allergic to them. Barbara from Barbara's Kitchen has helped me overcome this and has kindly supplied her information about egg substitution to help those of you who are in the same boat as myself. The first three recipes have also been kindly supplied by her.

Flour mix
For the GF/CF flour mix in all recipes I use a mix of

Ingredients
6 cups white rice flour
2 cups potato starch
I cup tapioca

Egg substitutes

To replace more than 1 egg is more difficult – it depends on whether the purpose of the egg in the recipe is for binding, leavening or both.

- If using egg whites – add up to 1 tbsp oil for each egg yolk to make up the fat
- 1 large egg is ¼ USA measuring cup in volume

Remember to check whether ingredients are allowed before using

- ¼ USA cup warm water = 1 large egg
- ½ tsp gluten free baking powder + ½ tsp xanthan gum + 3 tbsp water = 1 large egg
- 3 tbsp tapioca starch + 3 tbsp water = 1 large egg
- ¼ USA cup of ground soft tofu = 1 large egg
- 1 tbsp ground flaxseed soaked in 3 tbsp water = 1 large egg
- 2 egg whites + 1 tbsp allowed oil = 1 large egg
- ¼ USA cup of allowed pureed fruit = 1 large egg
- 1 heaped tbsp of gluten free baking powder + 1 tbsp allowed oil = 1 large egg
- 1 heaped tbsp of gluten free baking powder + 1 tbsp cider vinegar + 1 tbsp warm water = 1 large egg
- 8 tsp egg replacer + $^2/_3$ cup water = 3 egg replacement

Egg replacer powder

Ensure it is a gluten free brand. Often contains whey/lactose/ soya/citric – check labelling.

Dried milk powder substitution

- ½ cup dried milk = 1 cup + 2 tbsp liquid milk
- ¼ cup dried milk = ½ cup + 1 tbsp liquid milk

Water or juice do not contain as much protein as cow's milk. If used as substitution in dairy intolerance the mixture will not rise so high but the inclusion of a little extra xanthan gum may help.

If using an American recipe

- 1 stick margarine = ½ USA cup = 8 tbsp = 4oz = 100g
- USA Crisco = close to animal fat or lard/margarine mix

Barbara's miracle rolls

I couldn't include a recipe section without including Barbara's miracle rolls. These really have been a life saver to so many of us when our children are dealing with candida. Barbara has patiently endured many a phone call from me whilst I tried to perfect these without egg and I must admit I have produced many things before they eventually resembled rolls. I have found a good way to use up soggy miracle rolls is to pull them open and pop in chopped meat-balls or allowed meat and a bit of lettuce and call them pitta bread!

I have just about perfected these using baking powder and xanthan gum as egg replacer, and with egg they are a doddle and so delicious.

- Wheat/gluten/dairy/soya/yeast free and can be egg free
- Using American measuring cups and spoons

This recipe can also be used as a soft yeast-free pizza base - a higher temperature may be needed if using as a pizza base

Dry ingredients – gently mix together

1 cup white rice flour
¼ cup potato starch
¼ cup tapioca starch
2 tsp gluten free baking powder
1 tsp xanthan gum
pinch of crushed sea salt

Wet ingredients – mix together

1 large egg beaten (or egg substitute)
1 tsp cider vinegar (if allowed) or
  water
60g/2oz allowed gf/cf margarine
1 cup warm water (may need less if
  using as pizza dough)

Replacing allowed margarine with allowed oil:

- Replace allowed margarine with ¼ USA cup of allowed oil
- Reduce water to ¼ USA cup

Method

- Makes 4 large or 8–10 small rolls
- Preheat your oven 190°C (180°C fan assisted) 350°F Gas 4
- Gently mix dry and wet ingredients together with a spoon then using a hand electric mixer, beat for 2–3 mins – mixture should be quite 'sloppy' in texture.
- Use 4" diameter by 1" high individual fruit pie tins (Barbara can supply these) slightly oiled.
- Spread mixture to edge of tins as it will not automatically do this.
- Bake for approx 20 minutes – test to see if inside is cooked.
- Time may vary with your own oven – if using a muffin tray you may need to decrease cooking time for a smaller roll.
- Allow to cool before removing from tins.

For use as a soft pizza base spread the dough out on a greased tin. Add herbs to dough mix if allowed.

Barbara's 1½lb white-brown loaf recipe using liquid milk

For use in a breadmaker. Use American cups and spoons

Dry ingredients

2½ cups white rice flour
½ cup potato starch
½ cup tapioca starch
1 tbsp xanthan gum
2 tbsp sugar
pinch crushed sea salt
1 (2¼ tsp) sachet fast action
   dried yeast

Wet ingredients

3 large eggs (or egg substitute)
¼ cup allowed oil
1 tsp cider vinegar (if allowed) or
   water
½ cup allowed milk substitute
¾ cup hand hot water

Method

- Mix all the dry ingredients together in a bowl except the yeast.

- In a separate bowl mix all the wet ingredients together and place in the base of your bread pan.

- Gently place the dry ingredients (except the yeast) on top of the wet ingredients then sprinkle the yeast on top.

- Use normal bake setting with a choice of light/dark crust setting.

- When your machine first starts mixing I suggest you use a wet plastic spatula to help mix and turn over the ingredients to form a smooth sticky batter. Before closing the lid on your machine smooth the top of the batter with a wet spatula.

- On completion of the baking time – remove the pan from your machine.

- Remove the loaf and place on its side on a wire tray to become cold before slicing.

- This recipe freezes well and can be made into many varieties (Italian herb, banana, apricot, almond, ploughman etc).

- To make a brown loaf add 1–2 tbsp treacle/molasses (if allowed) to wet ingredients.

- To make a granary type loaf, add pine nuts, seeds (if allowed).

- To make a mock rye bread add 1 tbsp treacle/molasses (if allowed) to wet ingredients, add 2 tsp lemon peel and 1 tsp crushed cardamom (optional).

Chocolate crispy cakes

These rarely last long enough to set in our house. If allowed, add chopped glacé cherries or raisins

Ingredients

60g/2oz margarine
4 tbsp golden syrup
60g/2oz GF/CF drinking
    chocolate
14 tbsp GF/CF cornflakes or
    crispies

Method

- Melt fat and syrup slowly in a saucepan. Add drinking chocolate and heat thoroughly.

- Remove from heat and fold in cereal.

- Fill paper case and leave to set.

Sugar & Spice Madeleines

I decided to try these as I had an old Madeleine tin in my cupboard. They are now a firm favourite and use very little sugar. I often vary them by using coconut. Many thanks to the folks at GF/CF kids for this recipe. I have given the 'proper' way of making these but to be honest, I throw all the ingredients into my food processor and then pop the mixture into the Madeleine pan and straight into the oven.

Ingredients

¼ tsp salt
½ tsp nutmeg
2 eggs (or egg substitute)
½ cup sugar
¼ cup GF/CF margarine, melted

⅔ cup GF/CF flour
1 tsp GF/CF vanilla
1 tsp cinnamon
¾ tsp GF/CF baking powder

Method

- Makes about 2 dozen.

- Combine the salt and eggs (or replacer) in a medium bowl, and beat with a mixer at high speed until foamy.

- Gradually add in the sugar, beating constantly until the mixture is thick and pale (about 5 minutes).

- Mix the flour and spices in a bowl and stir well.

- Gradually fold the flour mixture into the egg mixture. Gradually fold in the margarine and vanilla.

- Coat a Madeleine pan with GF cooking spray. Spoon about 1 tbsp. of the mixture into each Madeleine form. (Instead of a Madeleine pan you may use a muffin pan, etc. filled not quite half full. The batter simply needs something to hold its shape.)

- Bake at 400°F, 200°C, gas mark 6 for 8 minutes or until lightly browned.

- Remove the Madeleines from the pan using the tip of a knife. Let them cool completely on a wire rack. Sprinkle with icing sugar.

'Five minute' Chocolate Cake

This is another recipe given to me by the GF/CF kids group and I just had to include it. Anything that takes five minutes is my kind of recipe. It takes even less time to eat and is delicious as a 'chocolate pudding' with ice cream

Ingredients

I cup sugar
I ½ cup GF/CF flour
½ tsp salt
¼ cup GF/CF GF/CF cocoa
    powder
I tsp baking powder

I tsp lemon juice (or I tsp cider
    vinegar)
¹/₃ cup oil
I tsp GF/CF vanilla
I cup cold water

Method

- Mix ingredients in order given. Pour into ungreased square 8 inch cake tin.
- Bake at 350°F, 180°C, gas mark 4 for 30–35 minutes.
- Cover with frosting or GF/CF chocolate.

Gingerbread cookies

Anna has these off to perfection. They are fine without the putting in the refrigerator, though much better with. Thanks again, GF/CF Kids!

Ingredients

1 3/4 cups GF/CF flour
1/2 tsp ginger
1/2 tsp cream of tartar
1/8 tsp salt
1/2 tsp GF/CF baking powder
1/2 cup GF/CF margarine (cold)

1 1/2 tsp xanthan gum
1/2 cup brown sugar
1 egg (cold)
1/4 tsp cinnamon
1/2 tsp GF/CF molasses

Method

- Makes about 20 cookies.

- Combine the rice flour, cream of tartar, baking powder, xanthan gum, cinnamon, ginger, and salt. Mix well.

- Cut in the margarine until the mixture is in crumbs the size of peas. In a small bowl, beat the sugar, egg, and molasses together.

- Add this mixture to the dry ingredients and mix until the dough pulls away from the sides.

- Form the dough into a flat ball shape and refrigerate for one hour.

- Dust some freezer paper or parchment paper (not wax paper) with GF/CF flour or confectioners sugar. Put the dough on the paper and sprinkle with flour or confectioner's sugar. Roll the dough to 1/4 inch thick and cut out shapes as desired.

- Bake at 350°F, 180°C, gas mark 4 for 12 minutes. Cool on a wire rack.

Peanut butter chocolate chip cookies

Another vote of thanks to the GF/CF kids group for these. They are a real hit for my children as they satisfy their chocolate and peanut butter cravings in one go! Again I have written the 'proper' way of making these but I put all the ingredients in the food mixer and they work out just fine.

Ingredients

½ cup GF/CF margarine
½ cup peanut butter
½ cup granulated sugar
½ cup brown sugar
I egg (or egg substitute)

I cup GF/CF flour
½ tsp baking soda
I tsp xanthum gum
I cup GF/CF chocolate chips

Method

- Preheat oven to 325°F, 160°C, gas mark 3.
- Combine and beat margarine, peanut butter and sugars until blended. Add egg (or substitute) and beat again.
- Combine dry ingredients (except chips) in a separate bowl then slowly add to the creamed mixture. Add chips.
- Spoon onto baking tray and bake for about 10–15 minutes

Homemade yoghurt

After excitedly opening the box when my yoghurt maker came, the children and I prepared ourselves to make yoghurt, only to find that all we needed to do was to pour the soya milk into the yoghurt maker and leave for eight hours!

I purée fruit or cheat and buy suitable puréed fruit and add to the yoghurt. It is usually eaten within minutes.

Ingredients

I teaspoon of yoghurt (GF/CF of
      course) to start the
      fermenting process
puréed fruit
I carton of soya milk
      (unfortunately I have yet to
      manage this with rice milk)

Method

- Put the yoghurt and carton of milk into the yoghurt maker and leave for 8 hours – taxing stuff!

Cream cheese

If you leave the yoghurt in a strainer for some time and add salt, this makes a delicious cream cheese.

I add garlic and chopped chives and the children love this warm on GF/CF bread.

Sauces

Tomato sauce

This is a basic sauce that I use for many recipes. In our house tomatoes are used sparingly as the younger ones like them rather too much!

Ingredients

2 tbsp olive oil
1 small onion, chopped
1 garlic clove, chopped
1 x 450g/15oz can chopped
   tomatoes

2 tbsp chopped parsley
1 tsp dried oregano
2 bay leaves
2 tbsp tomato puree
1 tsp sugar

Method

- Heat the oil in a pan over a medium heat and fry the onion until it is translucent. Add the garlic and fry for 1 further minute.

- Stir in the chopped tomatoes, parsley, oregano, bay leaves, tomato puree and sugar and bring the sauce to the boil.

- Simmer uncovered for about 15–20 minutes until the sauce has been reduced by half. Taste the sauce and adjust the seasoning if necessary.

- Discard the bay leaves.

White sauce

I use variations of white sauce for most pasta recipes. Add a little mustard, chopped ham, garlic, onion or whatever sits yours or your child's tastes and intolerances and pour over any GF/CF pasta for a quick and easy meal.

Ingredients

30g/1oz GF/CF margarine   salt
30g/1oz GF/CF flour   pepper
300ml / ½ pint milk substitute or
    for a more creamy sauce use
    single cream substitute

Method

- Melt 30g/1oz GF/CF margarine in a saucepan over a medium heat. Add the flour and stir continuously to form a paste.

- Slowly add the milk or cream and continue to stir till sauce thickens. If too thick add a little more milk substitute as required. Season to taste.

- To turn this into a 'béchamel' sauce. Put milk into saucepan with 3 peppercorns, 1 small bay leaf and 1 slice of onion and heat gently (not boil)

- Carry on as above using the cooled milk.

Chocolate sauce

Ingredients

2 tsp corn flour
2 tsp GF/CF cocoa powder
300ml/½ pint soya milk or milk
    substitute

1 tbsp sugar
knob of GF/CF margarine
vanilla essence

Method

- Blend the corn flour and cocoa powder with a little milk.

- Heat remainder of milk and when nearly boiling, pour onto blended mixture.

- Return to the heat and cook for 2 minutes, stirring vigorously. Add the sugar and a few drops of vanilla essence.

Poultry

Chicken nuggets (with or without herbs)

I am sure those of you with small children are worrying about how to replace chicken nuggets. I add herbs to make it a little more like Kentucky, but these can be omitted. The egg helps the coating to stick a little better but if, like me, you cannot use them, the milk substitute works nearly as well. I also use GF/CF breadcrumbs as a coating. They really are very simple and are handy in packed lunches.

Ingredients

Skinned chicken breasts chopped to desired size
I large egg (I omit this)
¼ cup milk substitute
¼ cup GF/CF flour
I tsp salt
I tsp pepper
I pinch dried thyme

I pinch dried oregano
3 pinches dried basil
3 pinches dried parsley
I tsp garlic salt
I tsp GF/CF baking powder – put in last
2 bags GF/CF crisps

Method

- Mix together all ingredients apart from crisps and soak chicken pieces in this mixture.
- Crush crisps as finely as possible in a separate bowl.
- Dip chicken in potato chips coating thoroughly
- Deep fry for 5 minutes
- Omit the herbs if required

Chicken Curry

Ingredients

3 diced chicken breasts
oil for frying
2 crushed garlic cloves
1 onion finely diced
1 tbsp garam masala
1 tbsp medium/hot curry
    powder

1 tsp chilli powder
2 tbsp tomato puree
150ml/¼ pint water
300ml/½ pint coconut milk
salt to taste

Method

- Heat the oil in a pan then add the onions and garlic. Fry until golden brown.

- Add the chicken, garam masala, curry powder, chilli powder and tomato purée. Mix thoroughly and fry for 5 minutes.

- Pour the water and coconut milk into the pan, stir the mixture together and bring to the boil. Reduce the heat and leave simmering for approximately 45 minutes. After this time reduce to suit your personal preference. Add salt to taste.

- Serve with boiled rice, GF/CF poppadoms and mango chutney if desired

- You may choose to add a greater quantity of coconut milk for a more creamy, richer curry. Reduce the quantity of water accordingly

Tagliatelle with chicken

This looks very complicated when written down but it is one of the children's favourites and really is very easy. The nuts can be omitted. As I have said, my sister is allergic to many foods, nuts being one, so it doesn't come naturally to me to use them. They are always a good source of protein if you or your child can tolerate them.

Ingredients

240g/8oz GF/CF tagliatelle
1 tbsp olive oil
salt
tomato sauce (as above)

Chicken Sauce

60g/2oz/GF/CF margarine
420g/14oz boned, skinned chicken
        breast thinly sliced
90g/3oz/blanched almonds (optional)
salt and pepper
white/cream sauce (see above)
basil leaves to garnish

Method

- Make chicken sauce by melting the GF/CF margarine in a pan over a medium heat and fry the chicken strips and almonds for 5-6 minutes, stirring frequently, until the chicken is cooked through.

- Pour the cream sauce over the chicken and almonds, stir well and season. Set it aside and keep it warm.

- Cook the pasta in a large pan of boiling salted water, first adding the oil. When the pasta is tender drain then return it to the pan, cover and keep warm.

- To serve the dish. Place the Tagliatelle in a dish and spoon the tomato sauce over it.

- Spoon the chicken and cream over the centre. Scatter the basil leaves over and serve at once.

Spicy chicken with peanuts

Again this looks a bit fiddly but really is easy and delicious

Ingredients

50 g/2oz unsalted
  peanuts/cashew nuts
1 green chilli very finely chopped
3 finely sliced chicken breasts
2 crushed garlic cloves
½ inch fresh ginger finely
  chopped
2 tbsp tomato purée

1 tsp ground all spice
2 tbsp GF/CF soy sauce
oil for frying
In a separate bowl mix :
2 tbsp GF/CF soy sauce
1 tsp sugar
1 tsp corn flour
1 tsp GF/CF vinegar

Method

- In a bowl mix the chicken, garlic, ginger, tomato purée, all spice and soy sauce. Cover and place in fridge to chill.

- Heat a small amount of oil in a wok or frying pan then add the peanuts and chilli. Fry until the nuts begin to change colour. Remove from heat and place them on some kitchen roll. Allow to cool. Don't discard the oil

- Heat the remaining oil to a high temperature in the wok or frying pan and add the chilled chicken mixture to the pan, tossing frequently. Cook for about 4-5 minutes. Ensure the chicken is cooked and stir in the mixed 'sauce' before adding to the chicken. Finally add the peanuts, stir frying for a further 1 minute, allowing the nuts to warm.

- Serve with boiled rice

Meat dishes

Goulash

Ingredients

90g/3oz GF/CF margarine
900g/2lb lean beef or any desired
    meat
2 tomatoes
1 tsp salt

2 tsp paprika
2 tbsp tomato purée
450g/1lb potatoes
1 green pepper
150ml/¼ pint soya cream

Method

- Cut meat into neat pieces. Heat fat in a pan and slice onion thinly.

- Fry meat and onion until golden, add tomatoes, tomato purée and season.

- Simmer for 30 minutes.

- Slice potatoes and add the green pepper. Continue to cook for 1½ hours till meat is tender. Stir in cream just before serving.

Corned beef hash

Ingredients

1 can corned beef
240g/8oz mash potatoes

1 egg, beaten (if you or your child is egg intolerant then use milk instead; we do)
1 tbsp oil
seasoning

Method

- Flake corned beef and mix with fat and beaten egg or milk. Season well.

- Spread evenly in frying pan and allow to cook slowly until underside is golden brown and mixture is hot.

- Fold like an omelette and turn onto a hot dish.

Moussaka

Ingredients

360g/12oz cooked potatoes, sliced
450g/1lb minced lamb or beef
4 tomatoes, skinned and sliced

chopped parsley
300ml/½ pint white sauce (see previous recipe)

Method

- Arrange half the potatoes in layers in greased ovenproof dish.

- Put the meat, sliced tomatoes and chopped parsley on top of the potatoes.

- Pour white sauce over potatoes. Cook for 25 minutes at 400°F, 200°C, gas mark 6.

Lamb and ginger kebabs

Have you ever attempted GF/CF ginger biscuits and ended up with a crumbly mess? This recipe uses up those or any other biscuits. Alternatively you can use left over GF/CF bread and add a little more ginger.

Ingredients

450g/1lb minced lamb
1 egg, beaten (I can use milk)
1 tsp garlic salt
pinch of pepper
180g/6oz ginger biscuit crumbs
pineapple pieces

cubes of green peppers
4 tbsp tomato ketchup
2 tbsp brown sugar
1 tbsp lemon juice
pinch ground ginger
1 tsp dry mustard

Method

- Combine lamb, egg or milk, garlic salt, pepper and ginger biscuit crumbs. Mix well and form into small balls.

- Alternate on skewer with pineapple pieces and squares of green pepper (though I use celery).

- Brush with mixture of ketchup, sugar, lemon and mustard and serve on a bed of boiled rice.

Fish dishes

I have my Dad to thank for the fishy recipes. I have a tendency to avoid fish out of habit (another thing my sister is allergic to) though my children all seem fine with it. Since Dad has given me these, I have found they have gone down well and are quick, easy and inexpensive.

Fish paté

Ingredients
cream cheese as above or
    suitable GF/CF soft cheese
tinned
    mackerel/pilchards/sardines

Method

- Simply discard the bone, skin etc from the fish and mix with the cream cheese.
- Delicious on warm GF/CF toast

Macaroni fish pie

Ingredients
450g/1lb haddock or desired fish
seasoning
150ml/¼ pint suitable milk
    substitute

300ml/½ pint GF/CF white sauce (I
    add parsley or dill)
knob of GF/CF margarine
240g/8oz GF/CF macaroni

Method

- Place fish in a saucepan. Season, add milk and margarine and simmer for 8–10 minutes until fish is just tender.
- Lift onto a plate, flake fish and retain liquid.
- Cook the macaroni.
- Use the retained milk to make up white sauce as previous recipe.
- Add fish and macaroni to white sauce, season to taste. Use a little more liquid if preparing beforehand.

Fish and onion bake

This one is another recipe that can be made at any time and popped in the oven when needed. The recipe can be varied using corned beef instead of fish and covering it with beef stock or GF/CF soup.

Ingerdients

450g/1lb cooked whiting or any suitable fish
450g/1lb potatoes
2 onions
150ml/¼ pint milk substitute

salt and pepper to season
fennel fronds or dill
parsley
knob of GF/CF margarine

Method

- Peel and slice potatoes thinly, do the same with onions. Break up fish.

- Cover the bottom of the casserole dish with sliced potatoes then add a layer of sliced onions then a layer of fish. Repeat the process and finish with a layer of potatoes on top.

- Season milk and add parsley, dill, fennel or desired herb and top with knobs of GF/CF margarine.

- Bake at 375°F, 180°C, gas mark 5 for 30 minutes or until cooked through.

Fish pie

Ingredients

1lb/450g/ fish (any to suit)
150ml/¼ pint milk substitute
seasoning
parsley
bay leaves

peppercorns
150ml/¼pint white sauce
450g/1lb potatoes, mashed
1 bag crushed GF/CF crisps

Method

- Put fish in a saucepan and cover with milk, adding peppercorns, salt and bay leaves. Boil or steam for around ten minutes. Alternatively pop in the microwave for around 5 minutes.

- Pour off milk, remove peppercorns and bay leaf then use the milk to make a white sauce (see earlier recipe) season sauce and add allowed herbs such as dill or fennel.

- Chop fish and place in dish, cover with sauce, top with mashed potatoes (for that added extra, add parsley) then sprinkle crushed GF/CF crisps and brown under grill.

Puddings and desserts

Sponge cake

Now I have a confession to make here! For my birthday cakes, sponge cakes and sponge for upside down puddings (see recipe below) I usually use dietary specialities cake mix. I get it on prescription. For those of you who have more time (and are not as lazy as I am), here is a basic sponge recipe, which can be adapted by adding GF/CF cocoa powder, coffee essence or whatever is allowed and takes your fancy. I make double this mixture and split between two 7 inch tins ready to sandwich together with butter cream and decorate to make a wonderful birthday cake.

Ingredients

120g/4oz GF/CF flour
1 tsp baking powder
1 tsp xanthan gum
120g/4oz GF/CF margarine
120g/4oz caster sugar

2 eggs (I substitute with 1tsp xanthan gum, 1 tsp baking powder and 6 tbsp hot water)
2 tbsp milk substitute
1 tsp vanilla extract

Method

- Cream together margarine and caster sugar, beat eggs or make up substitute and add to mix, fold in flour and add vanilla and milk substitute.

- Bake in 7 inch sandwich tin at 180°C, 375°F, gas mark 5 for 25 mins.

Pineapple upside down pudding

Ingredients

30g/1oz GF/CF margarine
30g/1oz brown sugar
1 small can pineapple rings

sponge mixture (see previous recipe)
glacé cherries

Method

- Spread margarine over the bottom of ovenproof dish. Sprinkle with brown sugar. Arrange pineapple rings and glacé cherries.

- Cover with sponge mixture and bake in moderate oven (325°F, 170°C, gas mark 3) for 50–60mins.

- Turn out and serve with GF/CF custard, ice cream or cream substitute.

Summer pudding

This is a really useful way of using up 'failed' bread or sponge cake.

The recipe can be varied in many ways using apples, cinnamon and sultanas, autumn fruits or any variation that takes your fancy.

Ingredients

6 slices of GF/CF bread or
    broken bits of GF/CF sponge
    cake
1 can of raspberries,
    strawberries or any fruit
    tolerated

Method

- Cut crusts off the bread (though I must admit I don't bother) and line the bottom of a pudding basin with it.

- Drain syrup from the fruit (whichever your child our you tolerates) and put the fruit into the basin. Cover with the rest of the bread.

- Put a layer of greaseproof paper on top and a weight and leave overnight.

- Turn out and serve with syrup from the fruit, soya cream or GF/CF ice cream.

Pear and shortbread log

Ingredients

Desired amount GF/CF
  shortbread or biscuits
I can pears or cooked fresh
  ones

120g/4oz apricot jam
I tbsp water

Method

- Bring apricot jam and water to the boil then place biscuits or shortbread on a serving plate.
- Cover with pear slices then add another layer of biscuit or shortbread and pears on top of that. Finally, add the last layer of shortbread or biscuit. Decorate with cherries and pour sauce over.

Waffles with eggs (with thanks to Carolyn from GF/CF kids UK)

I couldn't give an honest account of how we eat without including the recipe for waffles. These are so versatile and I really do make masses. We use them for an alternative to potatoes with lunch, cold as a snack in packed lunches, as 'tortillas' with dips and of course masses for breakfast.

All the children eat them laden with allowed spread and particularly love them spread with 'cream cheese'. Ben will only eat them plain of course.

Ingredients

90g/6oz GF flour

2 tsp gf baking powder

2 tbs allowed oil or 60g/3 oz GF/CF margarine

½ tsp crushed sea salt

2 eggs separated

8 fl oz GF/CF allowed milk

Method

- Sift dry ingredients into bowl.

- Whisk together eggs yolks and allowed milk and oil/melted margarine.

- Whisk egg whites to stiff consistency and fold into batter.

- Use good ⅓ US cup mixture for each waffle.

- Put into preheated waffle maker and cook – 4 mins will give you crispy brown – less for lighter colour.

Waffles without eggs (thank you Lesley from GF/CF kids UK)

I've found that if you make the mix, and use it straight away, the waffles don't go brown, but if you leave the mix to settle for a couple of hours, then they do!! They're also fluffier and tastier too.

Ingredients

1 cup white rice flour
½ cup potato starch
½ cup brown rice flour or other GF/CF allowed flour (eg tapioca starch)

1 tsp xanthan gum
2 tsp GF baking powder
1 tsp sea salt
1 tbsp olive oil or sunflower oil
1½-2 cups cold water

Method

- Mix with 1 tbsp olive oil, and 1½–2 cups cold water.

- Fresh mix needs 4 minutes per waffle, 'rested' mix only needs 2 mins.

- Brush waffle maker with oil after about 5–6 waffles.

3

A Week in the Life – Our Food Diary

An example of a typical week of meals and snacks may help you to realise that even with a large family and different tastes, there really doesn't need to be too much effort involved in cooking and preparing meals. This diary covers a week taken from the summer holidays so all the children apart from Matthew were at home for each meal. In school holidays, brothers and sisters and more able or older children can get involved in GF/CF baking. That has been the favourite pastime of my children this holiday so I have been able to sit back and virtually leave them to it. All the mistakes get used up in one way or another and the only rule is that they clean up their mess.

In my house we do mainly GF/CF cooking but still have 'ordinary' food in the house (though it is locked away) as my older ones are really too big for me to insist that they do the diet. If at all possible I would advise you not to have any offending foods in the house, but this may show you that the GF/CF diet can coexist with other diets if care is taken to use separate utensils, fat, etc. If I do cook a meal containing gluten, the three younger boys eat their GF/CF meal first, then the girls and Mat eat their meal. This is hard work and only happens if I haven't enough GF/CF food to go around.

I have a confession to make here! Despite all my efforts with my children, I am an excellent example of how NOT to eat! I tend to pick throughout the day and rarely sit down long enough to eat a meal. When I do, it is very late at night after the children have gone to bed.

A word of advice for other mums – take time to look after yourselves too. Your children need you to be healthy so be sure to either eat with them or have a decent meal later.

For our evening meal I always make a GF/CF meal but obviously feeding so many people makes it difficult to be able to suit everyone. For example, Ben rarely eats rice; it is something to do with the texture and I have not perfected exactly what suits him. Although he eats very well – in fact is an absolute pig – he still has his particular peculiarities, which I now understand and negotiate. After all, we all have our own little quirks, it's just that our kids seem to have them in abundance!

This particular week was at a time when the candida was well under control. Sometimes we have to restrict sugar and yeast again if the symptoms reoccur.

Monday
Breakfast

Gorilla munch cereal and soya milk (rice milk for Joe and Ben).

Mid morning

Walkers crisps and drinks of Peach High Juice.

Corn cakes with peanut butter.

Lunch

Beans on toast with dietary specialties bread. Girls had their regular bread.

Mid afternoon snack

Two or three buns courtesy of Anna, Joe and Luke's baking efforts (dietary specialities mix with 'chocolate' icing).

Drink of soya or rice milk.

Evening meal

Chicken curry (as per recipe) with boiled rice and poppadoms. Chopped baked potato and chopped chicken (put aside when I prepared the curry) for Ben.

Swedish Glace dairy free ice cream for all.

Drink of Peach High Juice for all.

Supper

Usually a case of anyone grabbing toast, biscuits or cereal but some days like today I am feeling particular charitable!

Mug of GF/CF hot chocolate and bowl of popcorn.

Bottle of milk for Ben.

Tuesday

Breakfast

GF/CF waffles (or flowers as Ben calls them). All except Ben have theirs laden with butter, GF/CF or otherwise and jam. Ben has his plain as he doesn't like mess.

When we have waffles for breakfast, I tend to be making them forever so I carry on after they have finished eating and freeze a load once they have cooled down.

Mid morning

Fresh orange juice and biscuits – Glutano shortcake on prescription for the boys and shortbread for the girls.

Bags of crisps.

Lunch

Alpha Bites and Swedish Crown meatballs with salad for all.

Yoghurts – homemade or Provamel for the boys and dairy yoghurt for the girls.

Drinks of Peach High Juice made with Danone Active water.

Afternoon snack

Bananas cut thinly and spread on GF/CF toast. Girls had banana toasties with ordinary bread.

Evening meal

Baked potatoes (not strictly true, they were boiled in their skins) with cheese for the girls and GF/CF garlic and herb cream cheese.

Salad (without the tomatoes for the boys).

Fresh pineapple juice.

Supper

Drink of milk and biscuits. GF/CF for boys and ordinary for girls.

Wednesday (a lazy day)
Breakfast

Rice cakes and peanut butter for all.

Milk or milk substitutes (soya and rice milk in our house).

Lunch

Girls made themselves toasties and boys had left over baked potatoes with tuna fish.

Yoghurts. Provamel for the boys and dairy for the girls.

Bags of crisps for all.

Afternoon snack

> More baking done by children. Bread was a flop so was put aside to make pudding with.
>
> GF/CF ginger biscuits were more of a burnt offering but disappeared quickly enough.

Evening meal

> Fish and chips from the local chip shop. The chips are cooked in their own oil and are definitely not contaminated and the boys have unbattered fish done in the microwave.

Thursday
Breakfast

> Omelettes for girls and Luke.
>
> Waffles out of the freezer for Joe and Ben who are allergic to eggs.

Mid morning

> Had an attack of guilt and put on my baking/cooking hat.
>
> Cooked masses of mincemeat and used some to make a bolognaise sauce and some for a shepherds pie. Also made a pint of white sauce with garlic and used half to make a lasagne and added ham to the other half.
>
> Made some bread which was successful this time, a chocolate cake (only a mix) sandwiched with coffee butter cream, ginger biscuits, peanut butter cookies and used up the failed bread to make a bread and butter pudding.

Lunch

> Everyone was feeling pretty sick after eating too many biscuits so the boys had rice cakes with ham and the girls had ham sandwiches and of course they managed a couple more biscuits!
>
> Drinks of pineapple juice all round.

Afternoon snack

Tinned pears.

Girls had an apple.

Evening meal

GF/CF pasta (I used rice and millet twists) and the remaining garlic and ham sauce for all.

Bread and butter pudding (which the girls and Ben thought was disgusting).

Supper

Slice of GF/CF chocolate cake.

Drink of milk or milk substitute.

Friday

Breakfast

Toast and jam for all – GF/CF for the boys and ordinary for the girls (don't forget to use a separate toaster).

Fresh orange juice.

Mid morning

GF/CF peanut butter cookies.

Lunch

GF/CF crackers ham and cream cheese (homemade) for all.

Tinned peaches and soya cream.

Crisps.

Cartons of cranberry juice.

Evening meal

Shepherds pie (made yesterday) and broccoli. Vegetables are not too familiar in our house, as I hate all of them so I forget to cook them and give salad and fruit instead. I do try to make an effort but even then it is not exactly appreciated!

Remaining slices of GF/CF chocolate cake for boys.

Chocolate biscuits for girls.

High Juice and Danone Active water.

Supper

Bowls of rice puffs for boys and rice crispies for the girls.

Saturday
Breakfast

Left over shepherds pie for the boys.

Cereal for girls.

Lunch

Off to Blackpool Bears with packed lunch of:

Swedish Crown meatballs

Cooked GF/CF sausages

Packet of corn cakes and tub of peanut butter

Bags of crisps

Cartons of pineapple juice and cranberry juice

GF/CF pretzels

GF/CF chocolate bars

Mars bars for the girls

Evening meal

Here's one I prepared earlier! I took these out of the freezer, as I couldn't be bothered today.

Fish and onion bake. Ben's needs to be mashed up to the equivalent of baby food to get him to eat it, but he does once I get it right.

GF/CF fruit crumble and soya cream for all.

Supper

Remaining GF/CF sausage sliced on rice cakes for boys.

Cheese toasties for girls.

GF/CF hot chocolate with milk or milk substitute.

Sunday

Breakfast

Awaiting a delivery of shopping so went to McDonald's for breakfast.

Boys had sausage meat, hash brown and fresh orange.

Girls had regular breakfast.

Mid morning

All fought over the remaining ginger biscuits and peanut butter cookies.

Lunch

Bags of crisps, corn or rice cakes and anything they can get their hands on (shopping has still not arrived!).

Afternoon snack

Shopping has come! Made Chocolate crispy cakes.

Bowls of cereal for all.

Gorilla Munch for boys.

Frosties for girls.

Evening meal

Roast dinner:

Roast pork, roast potatoes, carrots, broccoli, GF/CF Yorkshire pudding, GF/CF gravy.

Banana splits for all with Swedish Glace ice cream and chocolate sauce.

Peach High Juice with Danone Active water.

Supper

Chocolate crispy cakes for boys.

Chocolate biscuits for girls.

Milk or milk substitutes for all.

4

Packed Lunches

Packed lunches are often a source of worry when thinking of embarking on the diet yourself or when putting a school age child on the diet. With this in mind I asked Luke to write what he would recommend, though obviously adults may have slightly different preferences and those with added intolerances need to take those into consideration. One thing that often worries parents is that their child is taking the same every day. If we consider the fact that children with autism or AS do not like change, then it would seem that this is more our problem then theirs. If you have found something your child will eat and it is suitable, then go with it. It is far better to try to increase a child's 'repertoire' at home.

Luke's recommendations for packed lunches

A few things that are NOT good in a packed lunch

- Rice cakes are nice to eat straight out of the packet, but are horrible in packed lunches; they go all soft and smelly. Joe gets teased for having a smelly packed lunch.

- Another thing that really stinks in a packed lunch are eggs. My brothers are allergic to them, but I can eat them. The first time I took those to school, I soon cleared the table of people. Then again – maybe that is a good thing!

- Gluten free sausages can be bought in different shops depending on where you live, but absolutely reek in a packed lunch. Unless you really like it or have a very good sandwich bread I wouldn't recommend taking bread in a packed lunch. I know some people do like GF/CF bread enough to make sandwiches and maybe other countries, particularly America, may have some decent sandwich bread but, personally, I prefer it warm straight from the oven, or toasted.

- There are many part baked rolls that you can buy or get on prescription. These can be made into garlic bread by spreading butter and garlic on them straight after they come out of the oven but, again, I think that they are no good for packed lunches because they go all crumbly and are really hard to eat (and with butter and garlic on them, smelly too).

- I wouldn't recommend tea biscuits or crumbly biscuits as they get everywhere.

A list of things that ARE good in a packed lunch

- If you live in the UK you can get biscuits on prescription and I would recommend taking these to school, as they look more 'ordinary'. Remember that not all gluten free biscuits are casein free. I would recommend taking shortbread to school as the tea biscuits break into bits and get everywhere. Custard creams or chocolate chip cookies are even better but as we can't get those on prescription they are limited to having as treats.

- Corn cakes are definitely best in packed lunches and don't break up or go soft or anything.

- If you do take rice cakes or corn cakes, it is better to put a bit of whatever spread you want in a small tub and make up your 'sandwiches' when you are ready to eat. This way they don't go soggy.

- Crisps are one thing that manufacturers make a real mess of. Why they put lactose and wheat flour and all sorts in a potato product is beyond me! Watch out for MSG too (E621 or flavour enhancer; that's how they try to hide it). It gets everywhere. We have Walkers ready salted.

- There are loads of kinds of gluten free pastas. We like rice and millet, pasta and rice and maize. We sometimes take pasta cold with salmon or tuna mixed in as a packed lunch, and it really does taste delicious cold.

- There are meatballs that are GF/CF and these are good to have in at all times (not that they ever last long in our house). They are good for packed lunches – they tend to smell a bit, but are not too bad.

- 'Chicken nuggets' are good to take in packed lunches but, Mums, make sure that the coating is stuck on properly or it gets everywhere. If you can have tomato sauce then take a mini tub of it to dip them in.Peanut butter (if you are not allergic to it or cutting it out because of candida) is a good source of protein to have on crackers or corn cakes for packed lunch.

- It is good to take fruit in a packed lunch although I know that phenols and salicylates (don't ask me, there are links later!) affect some people so they have to cut out some fruit and vegetables and herbs.

- Soya yoghurts are good to take for packed lunches. I know Joe likes to take those because his other friends at school take ordinary yoghurts. He likes to be the same as others. Personally I am not bothered about that.

- Soya milk shakes are good to send in for kids who have 'milk time' and are good for packed lunches.

- Hi Juice is really nice, and it doesn't contain any artificial colourings or aspartame. It is hard to find drinks without aspartame. It does have sugar, so those who are doing the strict candida thing will have to cut this out for a bit at least.

- Pear juice is one of the best things for kids like Joe who react to phenols.

- GF/CF pretzels are another good thing to take. Other kids end up being pretty envious instead of teasing us. Much better that way!

5

Dos and Don'ts of the Diet

Just in case any of you are still having doubts about this, or like me, need to do a quick mental check list to make sure you are on the right track, here is one to help you on your way.

DO

- Give yourself a pat on the back. You have taken a positive step to improving your or your child's quality of life.
- Read all you can about it and understand as fully as possible. For UK readers I would strongly recommend reading Marilyn Le Breton's *Dietary Intervention and Autism* and also joining the AiA (see links). For US readers, though obviously much is applicable worldwide, I would recommend Lisa Lewis' *Special Diets for Special Kids* and Karyn Seroussi's *Unravelling the Mystery of Autism and Pervasive Developmental Disorder.*
- Be very sure that you want to embark on the diet.
- Decide when you are going to start and stick to it.
- Give the diet a decent trial. I would recommend a year.
- If you are going to try your hand at baking (most of us do) then buy in your ingredients and utensils ready for when you feel ready. For UK readers, Barbara's 'starter pack' from Barbara's Kitchen (see list of UK suppliers) really

does take the hassle out of this. It includes flours, measuring cups, xanthan gum and loads of recipes and advice. Barbara will also adapt any recipe to suit an individual intolerance.

- Make sure all the 'decks have been cleared' and your kitchen is organised to avoid cross contamination.
- Check for those last traces of gluten such as malt extract in regular cereals, they really do make a difference.
- Search your cupboards for hidden nasties such as msg (it gets everywhere) and aspartame.
- Make sure there is always plenty of available GF/CF food around. Prepare yourself for you or your child to feel bad during the withdrawals.
- Tell yourself that this is positive and will pass.
- Take time to look back and see how far you and (or) your child have come. This is a great source of encouragement.

DON'T
- Panic – this really is manageable.
- Let the lack of 'scientific evidence' put you off. The best way to prove or disprove this is to try it.
- Let others make you doubt your own instincts. You know yourself or your child best.
- Ever think you are alone in this. There is help and support available worldwide via the internet or telephone.
- Ever feel inadequate or that you don't know enough. To have come this far is a tremendous step and this is a steep learning curve. Take your time and use those around who are further down the biological road.
- Give in when you feel bad or your child becomes desperate through the withdrawals. This will pass.

- Ever think that 'just a little bit' won't do any harm. It certainly will.

- Presume that if something says gluten free it has not caused a reaction. Manufacturers are not required to list tiny amounts of gluten and casein.

- Worry about asking to read ingredients in shops, restaurants etc. People are usually very obliging.

- Leave 'off limit' foods around to tempt you or your child.

- Worry if you have an 'accident'. Just get through the reaction and learn from the mistake. We have all had them.

- Stop searching for answers. If removing gluten and casein has shown some improvement but there is still some reaction, then explore the possibilities of candida, a reaction to phenols or salicylates, and other intolerances. Following the Sunderland Protocol and getting guidance from a DAN (Defeat Autism Now) doctor is a good way to further explore the biological route.

6

Prescription List for UK 'Users'

Anyone restricting their dietary intake should have the support of their consultant, GP or dietician as care needs to be taken to check that the patient is getting adequate nutrients.

As Luke has stated, the theory behind the diet is just that, a theory, and to carry out clinical trials that are validated and considered reliable is most definitely problematic if not impossible. When working with people, particularly children, it is not viable to isolate and eliminate all confounding factors and therefore we must continue to work off positive anecdotal evidence as to the efficacy of the diet. I consider myself very lucky that I have the support of the boys' consultant, GP and dietician and I would like to thank them for their trust in my ability to know my children best and to do what is right for them. I would also like to thank my wonderful health visitor and best friend Mavis for always believing in me and supporting me. Words cannot say enough.

For those of you in the UK lucky enough to also have a supportive GP, it is possible to get GF/CF foods on prescription, though to decide which foods are suitable and useful for you or your child is a different matter. There is a vast array of GF/CF foods on the market and not all will suit you or your child's individual needs and intolerances.

In order to help with your prescription list, I have compiled a set of tables of prescribable foods. This list is by no means exhaustive and although, at the time of writing, it was accurate, companies do reformulate and change their products, so please check everything carefully.

The addresses and telephone numbers of the companies are in the suppliers list. Make sure to give these to your pharmacist otherwise you may have a long wait for your food!

Biscuits

Company	Produce	Gluten free	Wheat free	Dairy free	Egg free	Soya free	Corn free	Yeast free
Glutafin	Sweet	✓	✓	✓	✓	✗	✗	✓
	Digestive	✓	✓	✓	✓	✗	✗	✓
	Tea	✓	✓	✓	✓	✗	✗	✓
	Savoury	✓	✓	✓	✓	✗	✗	✗
Ener-G	Cookie	✓	✓	✓	✗	✓	✓	✓
Glutano	Maize	✓	✓	✓	✓	✗	✗	✓
	Shortcake ring	✓	✓	✓	✓	✓	✗	✓
Juvela	Sweet	✓	✓	✓	✓	✓	✗	✓
Dietary Specialities	Digestives	✓	✓	✓	✓	✗	✓	✓

Bread

Company	Produce	Gluten free	Wheat free	Dairy free	Egg free	Soya free	Corn free	Yeast free
Barkat	Brown sliced	✓	✓	✓	✓	✓	✗	✗
	White sliced	✓	✓	✓	✓	✓	✗	✗
Ener-G	Brown rice bread	✓	✓	✓	✓	✓	✓	✗
	White rice bread	✓	✓	✓	✓	✓	✓	✗
	Rice loaf	✓	✓	✓	✓	✓	✓	✓
	Tapioca bread	✓	✓	✓	✓	✓	✓	✗
Glutano	Wholemeal sliced	✓	✓	✓	✓	✗	✗	✗
	Par baked	✓	✓	✓	✓	✗	✗	✗

Lifestyle health care	White sliced	✓	✗	✓	✓	✓	✓	✗
	White unsliced	✓	✗	✓	✓	✓	✓	✗
	Brown sliced	✓	✗	✓	✓	✓	✓	✗
	Brown unsliced	✓	✗	✓	✓	✓	✓	✗
	High fibre	✓	✗	✓	✓	✓	✓	✗
Pleniday	Country loaf	✓	✓	✓	✓	✓	✓	✗
	Petit pain	✓	✓	✓	✓	✓	✓	✗
	Sliced loaf	✓	✓	✓	✓	✓	✓	✗
	Rustic loaf	✓	✓	✓	✓	✓	✓	✗
Dietary Specialities	Brown bloomer	✓	✓	✓	✓	✓	✓	✗
	White bloomer	✓	✓	✓	✓	✓	✓	✗
	Petit pain	✓	✓	✓	✓	✓	✓	✗
	Baguettes	✓	✓	✓	✓	✓	✓	✗
	Cobs	✓	✓	✓	✓	✓	✓	✗

Crackers and crispbreads

Company	Produce	Gluten free	Wheat free	Dairy free	Egg free	Soya free	Corn free	Yeast free
Bi-Aglut	Cracker toast	✓	✓	✓	✓	✗	✓	✓
	Cracker	✓	✓	✓	✓	✗	✗	✓
Glutafin	Crackers	✓	✓	✓	✓	✗	✗	✗
	High fibre crackers	✓	✓	✓	✓	✗	✗	✗
Glutano	Crackers	✓	✓	✓	✓	✗	✗	✗
Juvela	Crispbreads	✓	✓	✓	✓	✓	✗	✓
Orgran	Corn Crispbread	✓	✓	✓	✓	✗	✗	✓
	Rice Crispbread	✓	✓	✓	✓	✗	✓	✓
Valpiform	Crackerform cracker toast	✓	✓	✓	✓	✓	✓	✓

Flours and mixes

Company	Produce	Gluten free	Wheat free	Dairy free	Egg free	Soya free	Corn free	Yeast free
Barkat	Bread mix	✓	✓	✓	✓	✓	✓	✗
Dietry Specialities	White bread mix	✓	✓	✓	✓	✓	✓	✗
	Brown bread mix	✓	✓	✓	✓	✓	✓	✗
	White cake mix	✓	✓	✓	✓	✓	✗	✓
	White mix	✓	✓	✓	✓	✓	✓	✓
	Fibre mix	✓	✓	✓	✓	✓	✓	✓
Pleniday	Bread mix	✓	✓	✓	✓	✓	✓	✗
Orgran	Pizza and pastry multi mix	✓	✓	✓	✓	✗	✓	✓

Pastas

Company	Produce	Gluten free	Wheat free	Dairy free	Egg free	Soya free	Corn free	Yeast free
Bi-Aglut	Penne	✓	✓	✓	✓	✗	✗	✓
	Spaghetti	✓	✓	✓	✓	✗	✗	✓
	Fusilli	✓	✓	✓	✓	✗	✗	✓
	Macaroni	✓	✓	✓	✓	✗	✗	✓
	Lasagne	✓	✓	✓	✗	✓	✗	✓
Ener-G	Brown rice pasta (all types)	✓	✓	✓	✓	✓	✓	✓
Glutafin	Taglietelle	✓	✓	✓	✓	✗	✗	✓
	Spaghetti	✓	✓	✓	✓	✗	✗	✓
	Spirals	✓	✓	✓	✓	✗	✗	✓
	Shells	✓	✓	✓	✓	✗	✗	✓
	Macaroni	✓	✓	✓	✓	✗	✗	✓
	Lasagne	✓	✓	✓	✓	✗	✗	✓
Glutano	Spaghetti	✓	✓	✓	✓	✓	✗	✓

Company	Product	Gluten free	Wheat free	Dairy free	Egg free	Soya free	Corn free	Yeast free
Juvela	Macaroni	✓	✓	✓	✓	✓	✗	✓
	Spirals	✓	✓	✓	✓	✓	✗	✓
	Taglietelle	✓	✓	✓	✓	✓	✗	✓
	Animal shpaes	✓	✓	✓	✓	✓	✗	✓
	Spaghetti	✓	✓	✓	✓	✗	✗	✓
	Fusilli	✓	✓	✓	✓	✗	✗	✓
	Macaroni	✓	✓	✓	✓	✗	✗	✓
	Lasagne	✓	✓	✓	✓	✗	✗	✓
Orgran	Rice spirals	✓	✓	✓	✓	✓	✗	✓
	Gourmet corn spirals	✓	✓	✓	✓	✓	✓	✓
	Rice and millet	✓	✓	✓	✓	✓	✓	✓
	Rice pasta	✓	✓	✓	✓	✓	✗	✓
	Ris 'O' mais pasta	✓	✓	✓	✓	✓	✗	✓
	Ris 'O' mais lasagne	✓	✓	✓	✓	✓	✗	✓
	Ris 'O' mais spaghetti	✓	✓	✓	✓	✓	✗	✓
	Corn lasagne	✓	✓	✓	✓	✓	✗	✓
	Corn spaghetti	✓	✓	✓	✓	✓	✓	✓
	Rice spaghetti	✓	✓	✓	✓	✓	✓	✓

Miscellaneous

Company	Product	Gluten free	Wheat free	Dairy free	Egg free	Soya free	Corn free	Yeast free
Barkat	White pizza base	✓	✓	✓	✓	✓	✓	✗
	Brown pizza base	✓	✓	✓	✓	✓	✓	✗
Ener-G	Egg replacer	✓	✓	✓	✓	✓		✓
Innovative solutions	Gluten free blended flour	✓	✓	✓	✓	✓	✓	✓
	Xanthan gum	✓	✓	✓	✓	✓	✓	✓

7

UK suppliers

The lists of suppliers for both the US and the UK have been kindly supplied by the GF/CFdiet.com website.

Allergyfree Direct Ltd.
5 Centremead
Osney Mead OX2 OES
phone: 01865 722003
fax: 01865 244134
www.allergyfreedirect.co.uk
email: info@allergyfreedirect.co.uk/

Allergyfree Direct offers UK home delivery of a wide range of foods suitable for people suffering from food allergies and/ or intolerances. Virtually all products are VEGAN and GLUTEN FREE. Most foods are ORGANIC and we do not knowingly supply any containing genetically modified organisms.

Asda
customer service phone: 0500 100055

Reminder: Always remember when ordering from any manufacturers 'on line' you specify gluten and casein free

Barbara's Kitchen
PO Box 54
Pontyclun
South Wales
CF72 8WD
phone/fax: 01443 229304
www.barbaraskitchen.co.uk
GF/CF flour, xanthan gum (corn free) 'starter pack' and many recipes

Bi-Aglut
Novartis Consumer Health
Wimblehurst Road
Horsham
West Sussex
RH12 5AB
phone: 0845 601 2665 (lo-call)
Suppliers of a range of GF/CF produce many of which are available on prescription (see Appendix 6)

Brewhurst Health Food Supplies Ltd.
Abbot Close
Oyster Lane
Byfleet
Surrey
KT14 7JP
phone: 01932 334501
fax: 01932 336235

Suppliers of a range of GF/CF products including GF/CF cheese. Also suppliers of Pleniday products of which many are available on prescription (see Appendix 6)

Dietary Specialties
phone: 07041 544044
www.glutenfree-dsdirect.co.uk
GF/CF bread and cake mixes

Doves Farm
phone: 01488 684880
www.dovesfarm.co.uk
GF/CF flours and biscuits, etc.

Fresh Food Co
phone: 020 8969 0351
www.freshfood.co.uk
Retailer of GF/CF products

General Dietary Ltd.
PO Box 38
Kingston upon Thames
Surrey
KT2 7YP
phone: 020 8336 2323
fax: 020 8942 8274

Suppliers of different Ener-G, Tinyada and Valpiform products a lot of which are available on prescription (see Appendix 6)

Glutafin (Part of Nutricia Dietary Care)
phone: 01225 711801
www.glutafin.co.uk

Gluten Free Foods Ltd.
Unit 270 Centennial Park
Centennial Avenue
Elstree
Borehamwood
Herts
phone: 020 8953 4444
fax: 020 8953 8285

Suppliers of Glutano and Barkat products, many of which are available on prescription (see Appendix 6)

Goodness Direct
phone 01327871655
www.goodnessdirect.co.uk
Retailer of GF/CF Products

Gourmet Gluten Free Imports
phone: 02392 647572
www.ggfi.co.uk

Granovita
phone: 01933 273717

Green People
phone: 01444 401444
www.greenpeople.co.uk

Heinz
phone: 01942 214057

House of Eden Scotland
Retailer of xanthan gum, GF/CF products
Eden Place
Denhead, Kingswells
Aberdeen AB15 8PT
phone: 01224 749288
www.house-of-eden.co.uk
email: info@house-of-eden.co.uk

Innovative Solutions UK Ltd.
Cenargo International Freight Terminal
Calyton Road
Hayes
Middlesex
UB3 1AX
phone: 0845 6013151
phone/fax: 020 8756 3820
www.innovative-solutions.org.uk
Retailer of GF/CF flours, xanthan gum, pure flavorings.

Juvela
SHS International Ltd.
100 Wavertree Boulevard
Liverpool
L7 9PT
phone: 0151 228 1992

KP Foods UK
phone: 01530 412771

Lock's Sausages
West Lane
Edwinstowe
Mansfield
Nottingham
phone/fax: 01623 822200
Supplier of GF/CF/additive free sausages beefburgers and nitrate free
bacon and ham. Remember to specify this when ordering

Lifestyle
phone: 01491 570000
www.glutenfree.co.uk

Matthews Foods
phone: 01924 272534
www.pure-sunflower.co.uk
GF/CF margarines

McCains Foods (GB) Ltd.
phone: 01723 581230
Frozen potato products.

Meridian Foods Ltd.
phone: 01490 413151
www.meridianfoods.co.uk
Supplier of a range of organic and GF/CF products

Nestle UK Ltd.
phone: 01904 604604
Sweets, ice lollies and milk shake powder.

Nutricia Dietary Care
Newland Avenue
White Horse Business Park
Trowbridge
Wiltshire
BA14 0XQ
phone: 01225 711801
fax: 01225 711567
www.glutafin.co.uk

Suppliers of Glutafin and Trufree products, some of which are prescribable (see Appendix 6)

Nutrition Point Ltd.
13 Taurus Park
Westbrook
Warrington
Cheshire
WA5 5ZT
phone: 07041 544044
fax: 07041 544055
Suppliers of products under the name of Dietary Specialties, many of which are available on prescription (see Appendix 6)

Orgran UK
PO Box 3577
London
NW2 1LQ
phone: 020 8208 2966
Suppliers of a range of GF/CF food including an extensive range of pasta, much of which is available on prescription (see Appendix 6)

Parsonage Pork
phone: 01994 448255
GF/CF sausages, GF/CF, nitrate/nitrite free bacon

Pickerings
phone: 01603 742002
GF/CF Sausages

Plamil Foods Ltd.
GF/CF milk, chocolate, yogurt, carob drops.
phone: 01303 850588
www.plamilfoods.co.uk

Provamel
phone: 020 8577 2727
www.provamel.co.uk
GF/CF milks, yogurt

Pure Organics
phone: 01980 626264
www.organics.org
GF/CF burgers, minced beef, sausages

Safeway
customer service phone: 01622 712546

Sainsbury's
customer service phone: 0800 636262

Somerfield/Kwiksave
customer service phone: 0117 9359359

Tesco
customer service phone: 0800 505555

Trufree (Part of Nutricia Dietary Care)
phone: 01225 711801
www.trufree.co.uk
GF/CF breads, biscuits

8

North American suppliers

Abersold Foods
P.O. Box 3927
Citrus Heights, CA 95611
Vance's Dari Free (non-dairy beverage mix)
toll-free phone numbers within North America: 1800 2751437 or
1800 4974834
fax: 1800 4974329
www.abersoldfoods.com

Arrowhead Mills, Inc
Box 2059
Hereford, TX 79045
www.wholefoods.com
Gluten free pancake and baking mix

Adrienne's Gourmet Foods
849 Ward Drive
Santa Barbara, CA 93111
toll-free phone number within North America: 1800 9377010

American Spoon Foods
PO Box 566
Petoskey, MI 49770
phone: 616 347 9030 or 888 735 6700
www.spoon.com
email: information@spoon.com
Jellies, preserves, compotes, dried fruits

Authentic Foods
1850 W. 169th Street, Suite B
Gardena, CA 90247
toll-free phone number within North America: 800 8064737
www.authenticfoods.com
Mixes, baking supplies, pancake mix

Carolina Country Kitchen, Inc.
P.O. Box 1371
Flat Rock, NC 28731 1371
phone: 828 693 6549

'Cause You're Special, Inc.
P.O. Box 316
Phillips, WI 54555
phone: 1815 877 6722
www.causeyourespecial.com
email: foodallergy@rockriver.net

Cecilia's Gluten-Free Grocery
phone: 775 827 0672
fax: 775 827 5850
toll-free number within North America (orders only): 1800 491 2760
www.glutenfreegrocery.com
email: info@glutenfreegrocery.com

300 different gluten-free goodies from about 40 different vendors; some items contain casein – verify when ordering

Dining By Design

www.diningbydesign.com
phone: 402 327 8880
fax: 402 327 8496

Vegan online restaurant will provide nutritious meals for children with special dietary needs (specify food must be gluten and casein free). Prepared meals can be ordered on line and sent straight to your door. This is a service for parents who may not have the time or expertise to prepare meals at home themselves.

Edy's Whole Fruit Sorbet

Oakland, CA home office
www.edys.com

Ener-G Foods

5960 First Avenue So.
PO Box 84487
Seattle, WA 98124
phone: 206 767 6660
toll-free phone number within North America: 800 331 5222
fax: 206 764 3398
www.ener-g.com
Breads, pizza shells, donuts, mixes snacks, cookies, pastas, soup mixes

Food For Life Baking Co.

2991 E. Doherty St.
Corona, CA 91719
phone: 909 279 5090 toll-free phone number within North America:
1800 797 5090 or 1909 279 5090
www.food-for-life.com

G-FOODS,
Gluten-Free Bakers
3536 17th Street
San Francisco, CA 94110
phone: 415 255 2139
fax: 415 863 3359
www.g-foods.com
email: mail@g-foods.com

Gillian's Foods, Inc.
462 Proctor Avenue
Revere, MA 02151-5730
phone: 781 286 4095
www.gilliansfoods.com
email: R357BOBO@aol.com

The Gluten-Free Cookie Jar
P O Box 52
Trevose, PA 19053
phone: 1888 GLUTEN 0
www.glutenfreecookiejar.com

Gluten Solutions
phone: 888 8 GLUTEN
www.glutensolutions.com
info@glutensolutions.com

Online 'grocery store' that specialises in gluten-free and many casein-free
foods

Glutino (DeRoMa)

3750 Francis Hughes
Laval, Quebec
H7L 5A9 Canada
toll-free phone number within North America: 800 363 DIET
www.glutino.com
Huge selection of gluten free and casein free breads, pizza crusts, cookies, bars, crackers and all kinds of goodies.

Imagine Foods, Inc.

350 Cambridge Ave Suite 350
Palo Alto, CA 94306
phone: 650 327 1444
fax: 650 327 1459

The Gluten-Free Mall

www.glutenfreemall.com
Specialists in gluten free and casein-free diets. Food from 14 different manufacturers)
Specify when ordering that every product must be gluten free and casein free.

The Gluten-Free Pantry

P.O. Box 840
Glastonbury, CT 06033
toll-free phone number within North America: 800 291 8386
www.glutenfree.com
Mixes, baking supplies, pretzels

Kitchen Basics Inc.

Real Cooking Stocks packaged in cartons and are reduced fat and/or sodium. No yeast, gluten, soy, milk.
Also available by phone by the case: 1440 838 1344

Kinnikinnick Foods

10306-112 Street
Edmonton, Alberta, Canada T5K 1N1
phone: 877 503 4466 or 780 424 2900
fax: 780 421 0456
www.kinnikinnick.com
email: info@kinnikinnick

Kitchen Basics Inc.

Real cooking stocks packaged in cartons and are reduced fat and/or sodium. No yeast, gluten, soy, milk.

Available by phone by the case: 1440 838 1344

MenuDirect

Dietary Specialties
865 Centennial Ave.
Piscataway, NJ 08854
phone: 1888 MENU123
www.dietspec.com

Pretzels, mixes, condiments, baking supplies, cookies, pasta, snacks

Mona's Gluten Free

www.madebymona.com

Gluten free baking mixes

All products are GF/CF, with the exception of Mona's bread/roll mix

Miss Roben's

Box 1149
Frederick, MD 21702
toll-free phone number within North America: 1800 891 0083
fax 1301 631 5954

Pretzels, home-made mixes for cakes, muffins, cookies, pancakes, etc. snacks, cookies, crackers, pasta, puddings, wafers, GF/CF chocolate bits,

Order catalogue: www.missroben.com
email: info@missroben.com

Natural Noodles
PO Box 24006
Penticton, BC
V2A 8L9 Canada
toll-free phone or fax within North America: 1800 556 3339
www3.telus.net/noodles
email: natural@bc.sympatico.ca

Twin Valley Mills
RR 1 Box 45
Ruskin, NE 68974
phone: 402 279 3965
www.twinvalleymills.com
Sorghum flour (substitution for wheat flour in a wide variety of baked
goods)

Wilde Temptings
Gourmet Foods for the Food Allergic
phone: 1800 434 4846
www.wildetemptings.com
Gluten free pastas and mixes

The Really Great Food Company
PO Box 319
Malverne, NY 11565
toll-free number within North America: 1800 593 5377

Shelton's of Pomora, CA
Makes bologna & hot dogs both from turkey or chicken that is GF/CF,
corn free, soy free, no nitrates

Soyco/Soymage Foods
2441 Viscount Row
Orlando, FL 32809
www.soyco.com
Soymage dairy/casein free products

Sterk's Bakery
Vineland, Ontario, Canada
toll-free number within North America: 800 608 4501

Yorkshire Farms
Swedesboro, NJ
www.yorkshirefarms.com

Walnut Acres Organic Farms
toll-free number within North America: 800 433 3998
for a catalog
fax: 717 837 1146
customer service (toll-free number within North America): 800 344
9025

Westbrae
c/o The Hain Food Group/The Natural Food Division
255 W. Carob St.
Compton, CA 90220
phone: 310 886 8200 ext.112
email: westbrae@aol.com

Whyte's Darifree
www.darifree.com

non dairy beverage/darifree challenge. No rice, no soy, no dairy, no corn,
no gluten, no oils, no protein

9

Useful Information and Websites

Autism Research Unit
School of Sciences (Health),
University of Sunderland,
Sunderland SR2 7EE, UK
phone: 0191 510 8922
fax: 0191 510 8922

Allergy Induced Autism (AiA)
Membership Secretary,
8 Hollie Lucas Road,
Kings Heath,
Birmingham B13 0QL, UK
phone: 0121 4446450 or 01733 331771

HACSG (Hyperactive Children Support Group)
71 Whyke Lane,
Chichester,
West Sussex, PO19 2LD
phone: 01903 725182
fax: 01903 734726

International Health Foundation
PO Box 3494,
Jackson, TN 38303, USA
phone: 901 427 8100
fax: 901 423 5402

A range of information and books available relating to allergy and nutritional approaches to ADD ADHD. Send self addressed/stamped envelopes

The Feingold Association of the USA
PO Box 6550
Alexandri, VA 22306, USA
phone: 1800 321 3287

Alternative Therapy Network
1120 Royal Palm Beach
Blvd. 283
Royal Palm Beach, FL 33411, USA

Websites
Diet and medical website links

www.feingold.org
All about the Feingold diet, for the USA and worldwide

www.autismmedical.com
The Allergy Induced Autism website with useful links and forum

www.osiris.sunderland.ac.uk/autism/
The website of the Autism Research Unit containing the Sunderland Protocol: A logical sequencing of biomedical interventions for the treatment of autism and related disorders

www.autism.com/ari/

The Autistic Research Institute in San Diego. Provides much information about up to date research into autism. Organisers of DAN (Defeat Autism Now) conferences. Contains a recently updated list of DAN practitioners

www.autism.org

The Centre for the Study of Autism. Based in the Oregon area, the centre provides information to parents and professionals and conducts research in collaboration with the ARI in San Diego

www.gfcfdiet.com

American based GF/CF diet support group providing a wealth of recipes, idea and advice

www.gfcfkids@yahoogroups.com

A worldwide Internet based support group aimed at those implementing the GF/CF diet with their child or themselves. An essential source of information and support

www.gfcfkidsUK@yahoogroups.com

A UK based Internet support group again aimed at those implementing the GF/CF diet. Provides a valuable source of information for those in the UK

Autism, Asperger syndrome and AD/HD website links

www.oneworld.org/autism_uk

The National Autistic Society website

www.trainland.tripod.com/

A site with Winnie the Pooh backdrops, loads of links and loads of educational stuff

www.geocities.com/hotsprings/2125/hacsg.html

The Hyperactive Childrens Support Group which contains valuable information about AD/HD and related conditions.

Further Reading

Fenster, C. (1997) *Special Diet Solutions.* Savoury Palate

Hagman, B. (2000) *The Gluten Free Gourmet Baked Bread.* Owl Books.

Hansen, M. and Hansen, J. (1998) *E is for Additives.* London: Harper Collins Publishers.

Le Breton, M. (2001) *Diet Intervention and Autism: Implementing the Gluten Free and Casein Free Diet for Autistic Children and Adults.* London: Jessica Kingsley Publishers.

Lewis, L. *Special Diets for Special Kids.* (1999) TX: Future Horizons (distributed in the UK and Europe by Jessica Kingsley Publishers.)

Martin, J.M. (2000) *Complete Candida Yeast Guide Book.* Prima Publishing.

Semon, B. (1999) *Feast Without Yeast.* Wisconsin: Wisconsin Institute of Nutrition.

Seroussi, S. (2000) *Unravelling the Mystery of Autism and Pervasive Developmental Disorder: A mother's story of research and recovery.* New York: Simon & Schuster.

An Extra Note

Luke has written about the fact that the diet is not a miracle cure and nor would he want it to be. He is proud of who he is. I am proud of who he is.

One thing that the diet did not change for Luke was his insomnia. He has had massive problems both getting to sleep and staying asleep ever since he was born. Very recently he was still wide-awake at 1.00am and decided that he should take some medicine (amitryptiline) prescribed for both him and Ben to help them sleep. Luke was not the slightest bit tired and that particular bottle was prescribed for Ben so he presumed that he needed to take an awful lot in order to make him both go to sleep and stay asleep. I found him unconscious the next day and we owe his life to the intensive care staff at both Blackpool Victoria Hospital and Pendlebury children's hospital. I cannot ever express my thanks enough to the doctors and nurses who took care of him.

Luke has given me permission to write of this, knowing that other children may think like him and so I urge each and every one of you to look again at where medicines are kept and never presume that your child automatically knows the guidelines. Luke's thinking was logical and well thought out but yet those who do not know about AS would question that. I pray that as many people as possible learn from that one terrible mistake. I for one will never be quite the same again.

– Jacqui Jackson

Illustrations